Titan's Tales

and Other Dog Adoption Love Stories

By Julie Chalpan

Titan's Tales

ISBN 978-0-615-44671-4

Printed in the United States of America

Book design by Keith Chalpan

Acknowledgements

To our sweet Titan, who came into our lives and left his paw prints on our hearts. He is my best friend and the inspiration for this book.

May God bless all of the humans who touch the lives of rescue dogs.

Titan's Tales

Thank You!

Thanks to Pam Caldwell and the Gwinnett Humane Society who rescued our boy, Titan. We appreciate Pam every single day that we have with Titan. Growing up with cardiac asthma, I was allergic to dogs and all other animals. I thank God, my parents, Roma and Don Holmes, and my sister, Bonnie Chadderdon, for hanging in there with me so that I could outgrow my asthma and become healthy enough to have a dog and work with shelter dogs.

Thanks to all the people in this book who have taken the time to tell their story, and most importantly to adopt a dog. Thanks to all of the volunteers and staff at shelters, without whom we wouldn't know and love these remarkable dogs. Thanks to Titan's daddy, Keith, who I am so blessed to have as my husband, and also for his time and talent in designing this book. Thanks to my dear editor friend, Stephani Miller, for her tremendous editing skills. I am blessed to be surrounded by caring people and wonderful dogs.

Table of Contents

Table of Contents
(continued)

Foreword

The American Society for the Prevention of Cruelty to Animals (ASPCA) reports approximately five to seven million companion animals enter animal shelters nationwide every year, and approximately three to four million are euthanized (60 percent of dogs and 70 percent of cats).* The shelters and rescues continue to be overwhelmed with unwanted animals.

I started volunteering at the Gwinnett Humane Society in Georgia in the early 1990s. This is where I fell in love with dog rescue. My journey began when I adopted my second Jack Russell terrier, Pinky Piglet. She was an all-white Jack Russell terrier with pink skin because of flea allergies–so ugly, yet so cute, that you had to fall in love with her. After adoption we learned that Pinky was deaf and prone to seizures, which made us love her even more. She had 12 great years with us, and since that adoption we have rescued hundreds of Jack Russell terriers in addition to other breeds.

This is how we came upon Titan. Titan ended up in animal control when his owners turned him in because, they said, he kept digging out of their yard. He needed rescue to avoid euthanasia. I remember Titan was your typical spunky dog, a bit of Jack Russell terrier and beagle. His nose and tail went a mile a minute. The funny thing that I can remember is that to take Titan's picture, I placed him on top of the dryer so he would hold still. This book was written because of Titan and his owner's love for him and shelter dogs everywhere.

My passion continues today, and I have fostered and placed more than 200 dogs in my 16 years of rescue. We will never be able to adopt our way out of the overpopulation of dogs, but we can try to find homes for every adoptable dog. We must continue to promote and prompt legislation to pass strict spay/neuter laws.

With social networks increasing, adoption options have flourished. So please think twice before you buy a puppy. Why not adopt? It will give you rewards and love beyond your wildest dreams.

- Pam Caldwell

*American Society for the Prevention of Cruelty to Animals (2010). Retrieved January 9, 2011 from http://www.aspca.org/about-us/about-the-aspca.aspx

Titan's Tales

Titan

There he sat, separated from the other dogs from the Gwinnett Humane Society. Never mind that he is a Jack Russell terrier mix or that he is a "he," or that he didn't come up to me wagging his tail. From the moment I saw him, I knew he was our boy.

We knew we wanted a beagle mix. We knew we wanted to adopt a dog from a local organization. We thought we wanted a girl who was preferably through the chewing phase and already somewhat trained. We were building a fence at our new home so the dog would have plenty of space to play. We had been checking for months at the local PetSmart where they had adoptions on weekends and sometimes during the week.

Then, one Saturday on Halloween, while my husband and our friends were continuing the building of our fence, I ventured up to PetSmart because I knew in my heart it would be the day. Linda, a kind and loving volunteer, was outside waiting for me, knowing I would come for sure that day to meet Titan. There he was, a Jack Russell terrier/beagle mix. He was skinny at 17 pounds, about two years old, and very quiet. We learned later that he had just been neutered (no wonder he was so quiet). We also learned that he was rescued on his "kill day" from an animal shelter in another county. Pam, a volunteer with the organization with a big heart for Jack Russells, called the shelter two days earlier to ask if they had any small dogs. They told her about Titan, and she asked them to wait. She would be there to pick him up in 20 minutes. She knew that I would fall in love with Titan. That was 12 years ago and I will be forever grateful.

Don't get me wrong — Titan isn't perfect. In fact, it's his imperfections that make him so special. There are so many wonderful tales to tell about Titan, and the most humorous ones involve food. I will indulge you with only a few of his stories. I want you to meet Titan, along with so many other wonderful dogs, so many loving adoptive parents and so many dedicated volunteers and staff who work each and every day to rescue dogs like my boy and find them forever homes.

A Little More About Titan

Titan has always had food issues. We brought him home on a Sunday and by Wednesday we thought we had killed him, or at least made him very sick. This was my first dog and unfortunately I had not read his "owner's manual." Like all good parents, we showered him with gifts, love and affection. But the rawhide we gave him was definitely not a good gift for him, as we had no idea at the time that Titan had a sensitive stomach or that he would sit there and devour the entire thing. We were sitting on the couch watching TV, with Titan between us gnawing like a madman on the rawhide. We didn't notice it was getting smaller and smaller, or Titan's stomach was getting bigger and bigger. By the time we went up to bed, Titan had ingested so much of the rawhide that he was so bloated that he couldn't move. We picked him up, took him outside to do his business and carried him upstairs to bed. His belly was sensitive to our touch and we soon found the number to the emergency vet. They told us to come in if he got worse, but that everything should turn out—and come out—fine. We sat with him until 3 a.m. when it seemed like he wasn't in too much distress and we all went to sleep. The next day, Titan was just fine, and thanks to a dear friend who had learned from trial and error, we bought Titan his new favorite thing, a nylabone.

This was just the beginning of Titan's entertaining, and sometimes frightening, escapades with food. My husband Keith's favorite story is the first time he had Titan alone for any length of time. I had flown up to see my family in Michigan and he had gone off to a meeting. By the time he got home he was greeted by a very full dog, open refrigerator, and more cheese containers than you could imagine. He claims Titan not only opened the refrigerator to help himself to a snack, but opened the meat drawer, too. Titan ate partial containers of cream cheese, parmesan cheese, cottage cheese, lunchmeat, and anything else he could reach. He also left Keith a little present, since he could not get outside to relieve himself of his feast. Titan seemed perfectly fine. That night when Keith went upstairs and turned down his covers, there between his two pillows he found a block of cheese that Titan had buried for a midnight snack, in case his daddy had not come home to feed him!

We have too many stories similar to this one, like when we took Titan to see my family in Michigan, left a container of uncooked garlic rolls pushed back on the tall countertop to thaw, went out for a few moments to rent a movie, and returned to find them all gone and a "deposit" left in the dining room. Again, Titan was fine. And there was the time we were staying with Keith's dad and thought we had "Titan-proofed" the house, only to come back after a short while to find he had opened a bi-fold closet, tore open the Christmas wrapping paper, plastic wrap and tin to eat an entire pound of chocolate-covered mints. This didn't have quite as easy a fix, as after giving him a little hydrogen peroxide (recommended by the emergency vet so Titan would throw up the chocolate) he found it difficult to stop throwing up, which made him so dehydrated that he drank bowl after bowl of water. He seemed better by bedtime, until he curled up to me in a twin bed, and well, let's just say it wasn't pretty.

We did learn, after hiring a professional dog trainer for Titan when he was nine years old (we were slow learners!), that we could use Titan's food aggression to our advantage. Debbie, our wonderful trainer, had us get out Titan's crate, which we forewarned her that he detested. It's amazing how easily she could get him to go into the kennel with just a few kernels of food! And every day after that he would get in his kennel and sit patiently while we ate. He also learned commands like "down," "stay," "settle," and "leave it" — all with food as the incentive. She worked with him on his aggression to other dogs and cats, and it has helped through the years, and most importantly she taught us many things, including the fact that we were truly the ones who needed training!

Titan has mellowed over the years and is a truly sweet dog. He has always been sweet and loving with us, and now he loves his visits with the neighbors and other friends, and has made several doggie friends over the years. It's amazing how sensitive he is to what is going on in our lives. If I'm sad or sick, he knows and comes near me until I tell him it's okay, and then he quietly cuddles up to me. Following my two surgeries, I was concerned about Titan jumping up on me, but instead he was very gentle and loving, and again just curled up by my side. He is an incredibly smart dog, stubborn at times, and always my very best friend.

I hope you enjoy Titan's tale and the other wonderful stories in this book. I encourage you to adopt or foster a dog, and before doing so, to learn about different breeds and which dogs might be the best fit for your lifestyle. The more you know ahead of time, the happier your entire family will be, including your new pet. The unconditional love and pure joy a dog can bring to you and your family is not to be missed, and I am blessed to have Titan in my life.

- Julie Chalpan

Emma, Lacey and Abby

Abby, Emma and Lacey

My three sweet girls are Abby, a lemon (brown and white) beagle with a bit of cocker spaniel, Emma, a purebred beagle, and Lacey, a basenji, with maybe a little beagle.

Abby was the first dog I adopted, and she came home to live with Brandy, an eight-year-old golden retriever, and me. Abby and Emma were both adopted at the age of three from the Humane Society of Parkersburg in Parkersburg, WV, and Lacey, at two, was adopted from the Henderson County Animal Services in Hendersonville, NC.

I fell in love with Brandy as a puppy, and being my first dog she will always be very special. Since then I've seen the vast need for dogs to find homes; too many dogs are not spayed or neutered, so there is an unbelievable need for adoption. After I adopted Abby and Emma, I fostered several dogs for anywhere from two days to two months. I had thought about adopting a few that burrowed their way into my heart, but I already had two dogs. Then came Lacey

… and she had to stay.

Abby

I saw Abby at the mall in Parkersburg during an adoption fair. She was under the chair and didn't want to come out. She was white and light brown and very adorable. Her tail would wag, but she didn't come out. I knew fairly quickly she was "the one," and after a trip to the shelter, it was verified. She came outside on the leash for a walk. When I opened the car to get a sweater out that smelled like Brandy, she jumped up and settled into place with a look that said "I'm ready to go home, what about you?"

And then Emma

We were "thinking" about a third dog in the family and decided to visit the shelter. Curled in the back of a cage was Emma, shaking like crazy. She had been literally dumped in the middle of a cold February night in the shelter's parking lot and was suspected to have been abandoned by a dog breeder. She had only been in the shelter for eight hours when we saw her. We weren't allowed to touch her because she was so nervous. We adopted her on sight and brought her home a week later.

A house filled with three dogs is perfect, and after Brandy passed on I was ready for another family member. And that's when Lacey came into our lives.

And last, but not least, Lacey

At the Hendersonville shelter I was exercising several dogs off leash in the enclosed courtyard for a few days in a row. When Lacey came in as a stray, she had been found eating out of a dumpster at a Wendy's restaurant. I almost named her Wendy, but then thought her freckled legs looked like lace and named her Lacey. While all the other dogs ran like crazy through the courtyard, Lacey stayed by my side and followed me. Everyone knew she was pregnant, so I volunteered to pay to have her spayed and terminate the pregnancy. It turns out she had eight puppies in her 28 pound body, which was way too many, and the vet had to do more extensive surgery. The shelter folks asked if she could come home with me to recuperate in a quiet environment. I said certainly, and she hasn't left since then–except when she jumps the fence to chase squirrels!

In all cases the adoption process was a good experience. Adopting a rescue dog is the only way I will ever go. Three are enough right now, but when something happens to one of the current household members, I'll always go back to the shelter for a dog.

I volunteered at the Humane Society in West Virginia where I found Abby and Emma, and I now volunteer at the Henderson County Animal Services. I serve as the volunteer liaison, and I also do pro bono public relations, special events and promotion work for the organization. My favorite thing, though, is working with the puppies and matching dogs with the best homes possible.

My three girls are filled with tons of dog stories, too many to tell in one chapter! With Emma, it's her fear of everything and her need to hide under the bed during storms. Abby is the "food please" girl and shines her big dark eyes on you constantly in search of more food. Interesting, since she was bulimic for her first several months with us and threw up everything she ate. She also humped everything in sight until we broke her of that embarrassing habit. Lacey is a fast runner and has quite the appetite–for anything from rabbits to electrical cords. Her digging skills continue to become more enhanced, as she recently caught a mole in our yard! She also feels a great need to sleep next to me in bed.

Of course, I don't mind too much!

- Kathy Ziprik

Abby, Emma and Lacey

Akira

When we adopted Akira, or Kira as we call her, she was three to four months old. Her name is Japanese, meaning "intelligent," and boy, is she! We adopted Kira from the Spotsylvania Animal Shelter in Fredericksburg, VA. Everyone's best guess of her breed is she is an akita-German shepherd mix. Kira is our first dog.

Chris, my fiancé, and I had talked about getting a dog since we first started dating four years ago. We would visit PetSmart on adoption weekends every couple of months, or stop every time we saw someone in a pick-up truck parked along the highway with a sign about puppies for sale. But it was easy to walk away, because we both have very hectic schedules. Then last June we bought a new house, complete with dog door and nearly an acre of fenced yard, and then last December we got engaged, and I think it suddenly became much more realistic that we could have a dog. Chris grew up with dogs and I've always loved animals. I also thought it would be nice to have someone to keep me company when Chris is working overnight, and I love hiking and liked the idea of a partner on the trails.

Our biggest concern with adopting Kira was that she had already been spayed at her young age and we were worried about her health. We have learned that it is the policy of many shelters that all pets have to be spayed or neutered within about two weeks of adoption and that was a bit nerve-wracking for first-timers. It was also a little hard on the nerves walking into the shelter and hearing the barking dogs, who desperately want to find their forever homes, and it made us want to adopt them all. Part of me felt guilty for adopting a cute, cuddly puppy rather than an older dog that might not be so quick to get adopted, but Kira was ours from the first minute.

Chris especially knew immediately that Kira was going home with us. When we arrived at the shelter there was a couple in the process of adopting a little puppy, and while I was waiting to talk to one of the volunteers, I could feel Chris becoming restless beside me. When I overheard them mention that it was likely an akita-mix puppy, I understood why, because he had been wanting just that for a while and apparently had realized that is what the puppy beside us was. When we went into the kennel portion, Chris disappeared. I made my way down the line of dogs, petting each of them, and eventually met up with him at the fourth cage down, where a puppy was licking his fingers. "This is the one," he said. It was Kira's brother we saw out front, and we later learned that she and three male littermates had been discovered on the side of the road four days earlier. She was the last one left.

I was still a bit in disbelief about the whole process, even though it was something we had been discussing for a while, so I made Chris look at every other dog there. In fact, we had gone with the intention of looking at a specific dog, and we saw that Rhodesian ridgeback there, but she was just another dog, not our dog. Then we went back and played with the puppy. Kira just wanted to curl up and hide beneath our legs as we squatted on the ground. Chris refused to give her back to the volunteers!

I didn't realize how much I wanted her until Chris was paying and signing her paperwork and I was holding the leash in the waiting room. She was very timid, trying to hide beneath the chairs, but then these three little kids came over and held out their hands and she went right out to meet them, just sweet as could be. She loves kids, and I thought at first it's because they were about her size, but now I think it's just because she feels very protective. I liked how brave, curious and friendly she seemed.

I'm sure everyone says this about their dog, but she is super-smart. We enrolled her in the intermediate training class when she was five months old because she was so quick to catch on to all the basics—sit, stay, roll over, etc. We're waiting for the next advanced class to get going to enroll her in that. She's also extremely affectionate. There's no beating a "Kira hug" when she will come over to you if you're sitting on the ground and awkwardly lean her head down against your leg and snuggle before the rest of her body hits the ground with a thud.

Kira loves tug-of-war and finally has mastered fetch. And she's still fantastic with kids. We recently rented a beach house with several other couples, and there were a couple of kids there ranging from one to four years old. She loves being around toddlers—she would sit next to the little boy and they would share toys, and she would follow him around when he started crawling, and he could lean and tug all over her and she wouldn't bat an eye. One of the things Chris loved and I worried about with an akita was that they have a reputation for being overly protective of their owners, which is why I think I'm so pleased that she's social. And she definitely does like to keep an eye on us.

My experience with volunteering at a shelter is limited to college. I volunteered with an SPCA one semester and at the Spotsylvania Animal Shelter for another semester when I was in college. At the shelter, they have a section where they spay and neuter the animals before they're allowed to go to their new homes. I would help clean out the cages after the animals left for the day. Not exactly fun work, but I enjoyed it because I got to spend some time with the dogs and I knew at the end of the day they were going to their forever home. Those are good memories, and we are so glad that we have given Kira her forever home.

- Megan Headley and Christopher Rinderknecht

Angus

Angus, a great Dane, was a big dopey guy – in a good way. He came into our lives and we will never be the same. He was surrendered by a college student. We heard about him from a friend of my husband's, Dr. Samson, who told us that a one-year-old great Dane had been at the shelter for weeks, had awful mange, and needed a good home. We had never heard of a great Dane being in a shelter before and we thought that we should go and look at him, although I'm not sure why. We were not looking for a second dog, because at the time we had another great Dane named Samson, who was seven. I think we were just drawn to Angus' sad story.

I visited Angus at the Coulee Region Humane Society in La Crosse, WI. I went to look at him during my lunch break, called my husband, and we agreed to put in an application. During the interview, Angus and I played with a tennis ball and he seemed very sweet, leaning on my leg to look up into my face. His skin problems were apparent but didn't seem to trouble him too much. We got a call an hour later. We were his fifth applicants, but because we already had a Dane in the family and we have a big lot in the country, they felt ours was the right home. This was the first time we adopted from an organization. I now volunteer with a similar organization in the county where I live – Vernon County Humane Society – and now we always adopt shelter dogs.

Looking back, adopting Angus seemed like fate. My husband and I both feel that we were led to adopt him. It seemed like one step followed the other and we did not question any of them. We just kept moving forward.

We knew Angus had some health problems. His mange was not the usual mange you think of caused by mites, but a different kind, which we would learn more about later. Looking at his pimply skin, red leathery ears and tomato-red feet, we knew there were challenges ahead. We took him to our vet who treated him with antibiotics, the standard treatment at the time, which apparently was killing the flora in his body. His digestive system was declining and we became more and more worried. He required surgery after four days of vomiting; he had a lot of undigested food in his intestines. We then took him to a holistic vet who deduced right away that he had food allergies. We learned how to feed him, making whole foods for him to eat, and he healed slowly. His ears cleared up, his skin healed and his itching disappeared. He was healthy and happy for probably the first time in his life.

As he healed, his personality began to shine through. He was a big love bug, built more like a mastiff, with soulful eyes. He had more charisma than any other dog I've ever known. Our friends and family adored him.

I know these are all supposed to be stories with happy endings, and really this one is, too, even though our Angus is gone now. What's remarkable is that the last night of his life he tried very hard to tell me something. It was probably the most amazing moment that I have ever had with any pet. After work that day I let the dogs out and Angus lay down in the grass, sphinx style. I sat down next to him and he looked right into my eyes and barked about 40 times in very measured barks. Angus tried, with everything he had, to give me a loving message, and I tried very hard to decode it, returning his steady gaze while he barked on and on. It began to make sense the next day, when we learned he had advanced cancer and we had to say goodbye. I believe he was trying to tell me that he was dying and that he loved us, and that we will be together again one day.

There is something really special about the devotion we share with our animals.

- Anna Nirva

Anna's Charitable Organization

Anna Nirva, Angus' mom, started a non-profit organization called Sunbear Squad. Sunbear Squad is a non-profit humane organization that seeks to prevent pet and domestic animal suffering by educating and empowering individuals to advocate for animals in a positive and assertive manner. One person helping and one animal helped build a more kind and compassionate world.

The organization was named after Sunbear, who was an 18-month-old male chocolate Labrador retriever in a West Virginia town. One summer day in 2002, his owner locked him in a dark townhouse laundry room, with no food or water, and walked away. His owner intended to give him to a farm family, but communication broke down and nobody picked up poor Sunbear. Sunbear was found six weeks later and died three days afterward, despite valiant efforts by the veterinary staff. His owner was finally found and sentenced to the fullest extent of the law. Because of Sunbear, West Virginia legislature enacted much stricter laws on animal neglect and abuse and continues to improve animal cruelty legislation.

When the Humane Society of the United States published articles about Sunbear's ordeal and his owner's sentencing, Anna resolved to publish a web site in Sunbear's memory that would encourage people everywhere to help companion animals in distress, because Sunbear did not get help.

Beans

Beans was six years old when I adopted her. She is an adorable Jack Russell terrier mix and came to me from a shelter in Rhode Island. I wanted to give a loving home to an at-risk dog – it is just the right thing to do! The adoption process was amazing and I brought my girl home the same day.

My family adopted a dog when I was a child, and Beans was the first dog I adopted on my own. A friend suggested I go to the shelter to take a look at dogs. I was really only entertaining the possibility of getting a dog, so I thought it wouldn't hurt to take a look. The second I saw Beans, I knew she was my dog. She looked so tiny in the big kennel. Her little tail started to wag and she began to lick my hand through the cage. I had to take her home.

When I turned in my application, I became crestfallen when the woman at the desk told me that a family was supposed to be coming in that day to pick up Beans. How could they? She was my dog! The woman told me she would make a phone call to check on the status of the pick-up. Much to my delight and amazement, the family had decided that Beans wasn't for them. I took her home with me that day.

Beans is an amazing, funny little girl. She is incredibly smart and mischievous. Once when I was having a particularly tough day and had become emotional, I sat on the floor in my living room. Beans came over, climbed into my lap and put her paws on my shoulders – literally giving me a hug! She is such a blessing. I'll definitely adopt another dog someday and I make charitable contributions to SPCA as a 'thank you' for Beans and for other dogs out there that need homes.

- Nancy Widman

Bella

Bella came into my life when she was 11 months old, and as sweet and large as she could be. A great Dane was quite an addition to our family. We already had Madison, a seven-year-old cocker spaniel, and Brutus, a nine-year-old Yorkshire terrier.

Bella came from Great Dane Rescue Inc., Michigan where we had been members of the rescue for about three years prior to adopting her. At first we just helped out with transporting and home checks. Then we began fostering. We enjoyed fostering great Danes and had a great time experiencing the differences in the different colored great Danes. Each color category has different traits and it was fun to explore the differences.

Bella was our eighth foster great Dane. When I first saw her I fell in love, and after fostering so many Danes, it was surprisingly the first time this happened to me. I didn't want to believe it, so I kept it to myself until we watched her behavior and saw how she got along with my other dogs. She was so beautiful and such a sweet puppy she became ours pretty quickly.

It is so important to give an unwanted dog an opportunity to experience a loving home. And the added bonus from fostering and/or adopting dogs is that most of them come potty trained! I would adopt another dog in a heartbeat. Even though we had been fostering dogs for a while, this was my first adoption experience. In the past we had enjoyed going to the local Humane Society and looking at the dogs, but we had never so quickly fallen in love.

Bella's Quirks

Bella, being an especially large dog, makes a huge mess when she drinks. Half of the water stays in her jowls and then streams out all over the floor as she walks away from her bowl. We keep a full sized towel on the floor so we can drag it around and wipe up her mess. If she picks up something she shouldn't (like Q-tips for instance), when questioned she will immediately bring it to me and waits for me to open her mouth and pluck it out.

Bella loves to be outside and is ecstatic about our back yard. She will run full force from one end to the other around the hot tub and back to the other end. She will play this game over and over and over until she is completely exhausted. She also plays with her toys outside all by herself. Another game she often plays is running from one end of the yard to the other carrying her toy and throwing it up in the air and pouncing on it. At bedtime, if she is lucky enough to get to sleep with me, she will jump on the bed and face me as I attempt to get into bed. She puts her head down and tries to bulldoze me off and keep me from getting under the covers.

A mylar balloon is the one thing that Bella is afraid of and we found this out one Mother's Day. My youngest daughter bought my mom, sister and me Mother's Day balloons, and when my sister went to leave she took her balloon, and Bella just about knocked people over trying to get out of the way. She then proceeded to bark and growl at mine on random occasions. She has now learned to trust me enough to lower a balloon down for her to sniff.

The Rest of the Family

My other two dogs have interesting stories, too, although neither of them were adopted. Brutus, the Yorkie, was born at our house on Valentine's Day 2001. I had raised a couple of litters of Yorkies. Madison's story is quite different. I met a couple that told me that their cocker spaniel (who was covered in fleas) had just given birth to eight puppies and they didn't have the money to dock the tails. They told me that three of the puppies weren't doing so well and I felt the need to offer my help to them. Since I had experience raising puppies, I told them that I would take the momma and her puppies and attempt to nurse the three small ones to health. They brought them over to me the day after she had them and I went to work trying to save the three failing pups. The five healthy puppies survived and we kept them for eight weeks but I was determined NOT to keep any of them permanently. You can guess what happened. That is how Madison came to live with us.

- Loraine Blake Smikle

Bonnie Bleu

We adopted Bonnie Bleu from the Hilton Head Humane Association. A four-year-old American pit bull, Bonnie Bleu has literally danced her way into our hearts.

We had just unexpectedly lost Philly, our pit bull/Labrador retriever mix of over 10 years. Philly was left at our door as a puppy, and she was a wonderful girl. When she passed, we decided we wanted to share our home with an older dog instead of getting a puppy because we wanted a fully grown sister for Beaux, our 10-year-old weimaraner. In addition, in Philly's memory, we wanted to give a chance to a dog that did not already have a home.

First Adoption

We set out on a Saturday to the Hilton Head Humane Association on Hilton Head Island, SC. Having never adopted a dog (although I have been known to take in strays), the adoption experience was much easier than I thought it would be. They allowed, and even encouraged, us to bring Beaux to be a part of the experience.

The plan was for the three of us, including Beaux, to go and just look at the dogs there. I was a bit closed to the prospect of adopting a dog because I thought it would be painful to make a choice knowing that others would have to stay. But when I saw Bonnie Bleu smile, I knew she was ours. I think that she knew, too.

Later I learned that Bonnie Bleu had been returned to the shelter that day because her previous adopter took her home and she was attacked by their other dog. So she had been taken to the shelter twice. When I posted Bonnie's picture on the Hilton Head Humane Association's Facebook page, Bonnie's last adopter saw the post and asked about her well-being. She shared with me how she cried when she had to return Bonnie, but she feared for Bonnie's safety after the other dog attacked her. She thanked me and asked me to please send pictures of Bonnie so she could still share in her adoption. Since then, Bonnie has acquired two families, because our new friend has given me lots of insights about Bonnie's breed, as she has raised American pit bulls all of her life.

Happy Girl

Bonnie Bleu has been a joy. Having her with us is like unwrapping a new present every day. She has a unique personality and is so full of life. Because we did not see her develop as she grew, it is a gift to discover each day. We call her "corndog" because of the happy dance that she does when she is having fun, and her sweet smile is contagious!

Unfortunately, I don't have the fortitude to volunteer with a rescue organization. I wanted to be a veterinarian as a child until I realized that I might not be able to save all of the animals in my care. I do not let go easily. I have great respect for those who do work in rescue organizations and am grateful for the wonderful adoption experience we had at the Hilton Head Humane Association.

- Diana Bourgeois

Bonnie Bleu and Beaux

Buster

I remember the day we adopted Buster like it was yesterday. Buster was my first pet and was adopted in Atlanta, GA. He was a three-year-old black Labrador mix, with the mix being basset hound, since he had short little legs and his paws turned out.

Not having been a pet owner before, I wasn't knowledgeable about rescue dogs versus purebred dogs. My husband, on the other hand, grew up with dogs, all of whom he adopted from humane societies or shelters. He believes very strongly in rescuing dogs, so I followed his lead. Actually, truth be told, we never made a decision to go out and adopt a dog. Well, I didn't anyway.

Two weeks after we were married and one week after returning from our honeymoon, my husband suggested we visit the shelter to just look at the dogs. About four hours later we returned home with Buster.

We walked into the shelter and I was taken by a box

full of roly-poly puppies. We played with them for a bit, then headed back to see the adult dogs. I told the volunteer I thought I wanted a golden retriever. She let me know they had one, but he was already adopted. The volunteer showed us the golden, then she left us to look around on our own.

I played with the golden a bit while my husband walked up and down the aisle. He stopped at the pen next to the golden, picked up the dog information clipboard and gasped. I looked at him and he looked down at this adorable black Lab mix. The paperwork said his name was Buster and he was three years old. What was interesting was that my husband had recently told me that he would love a black Lab, and he wanted to name him Buster. It was definitely meant to be!

We took Buster into a visiting room to play with him. He was so sweet, jumping up on my husband, rubbing on his legs and rolling over to show his belly. He had obviously suffered no trauma from being left at the shelter and he was in excellent health. His paperwork revealed that he had only been there since Thursday and it was a Saturday. His previous owners had left him because they lived in a high-rise apartment building and he was too "high-spirited" for such a confined space.

I knew I liked dogs, but I was still a little nervous around Buster, not having owned a pet. He sniffed me, licked my leg and then nonchalantly peed on my feet. My husband and the volunteer howled with laughter and said he had christened me. When my husband stopped laughing he gave me a look and I knew that Buster was going home with us.

The volunteer interviewed us for more than an hour about our home, our backyard, our travel habits, etc. It was much more rigorous than I expected. In hindsight, it's clear they were very committed to placing their animals in good homes.

We bought a leash and collar from the shelter's store,

threw an old towel from the trunk across the backseat, and took Buster home. We introduced him to his new yard and spent hours sitting on the grass just getting to know him. We made an emergency trip to the grocery store for dog food, a water bowl and a bag full of toys. The next day an Orvis catalog arrived in the mail and I ordered Buster his first of many bright red Orvis embroidered collars.

Buster's First Night

The first night at home we weren't sure what to do with Buster. Leave him in the yard? Let him sleep in the house? We were told he was housebroken, but we just didn't know him yet and weren't sure what to do. We decided to let him sleep in his new dog house in the backyard.

My husband woke up first the next morning and went outside only to discover that Buster had dug out under the fence in the night. I was devastated and cried and cried for him. Within about five minutes we found him, curled up asleep at the front door, waiting to be let in. He never spent a night outside after that. He was always snuggled into his red plaid doggie nest.

Jackpot!

Over the next few months we discovered that we had hit the canine jackpot. Not only was Buster housebroken, he was very well trained and learned new things almost immediately. We never used a crate with him, as he would sit or stay anywhere in the house or yard until we released him. He never had any accidents in either of the two houses we lived in with him. He was sweet, he never jumped (after we trained him out of it), he walked well on a leash, and he listened to us.

Although Buster is no longer with us, he'll always be

the best and sweetest dog for which I could ever have hoped. There's something very special about your first dog. He filled my life with love and so many stories including letting the children hold his tail, peeing in my brand-new Mazda, refusing to pee in the snow on the rare occasions it snowed in Atlanta, sleeping under the crib for a month, and sleeping under my desk on top of my toes.

And then came Scout

We knew we could never replace Buster, but when our family was ready for another dog we adopted Scout from Labrador Friends of the South (LFS). I handled pro bono media relations for LFS for about two years. Scout is a chocolate Lab mix. My husband says the mix is coonhound since she doesn't bark, she bays. She was a three-month-old abandoned puppy LFS stumbled upon in Alabama while rescuing another dog. I had been talking with LFS volunteers telling them we were looking for a chocolate Lab puppy and they called me from Alabama, emailed a photo of Scout, and it was a done deal. She is now five years old and remains a wide-open bundle of doggie energy. She is wonderful with both of our children. She is protective and she loves to sleep in one of the children's beds. We tell her every day that she's the most perfect brown dog in the world. Buster, of course, was the most perfect black dog.

- Kim Drew

Scout

Cami

After losing our beloved dog Willow, later that fall my other dog, Conner, and I visited a Georgia Humane Society adoption event. Cami was just twelve weeks old when she came into our lives. She was the "Big Kahuna" of her litter– not in size, but in temperament. When challenged, she was defiant and even aggressive. She would lord over her litter mates, steal their toys, and gloat over her treasure horde. For some reason, I was attracted to her as a "hard case" and Conner really liked her. With Cami, a golden retriever/yellow Labrador retriever mix, it was love at first sight for Conner and me, even if she seemed to have all the characteristics of a true hellion. Three years later we now have three full-time dogs, and the pack has helped foster 30 rescue dogs.

It was a smooth and professional adoption process, including an interview-application form, vet references, and a home check. I had owned dogs for ten years and had fostered a bearded collie named Mac, so I was an experienced dog owner. I finally learned about the plight of companion animals and how I could actually help in ways other than a monetary donation. That just proves you can teach an old dog a new trick! Later I adopted Chip, another foster, bringing our pack to three.

Kamikaze Camille, her full name, grew into an under-sized Lab mix. At just 55 pounds fully grown, she can be the sweetest dog in the world. She smiles all the time and is normally an easy going dog, so we call her "Cami." Yet she can be fierce, so we also call her "Kami" for her Kamikaze mode. She simply doesn't hold with aggressive dogs who assert themselves as alpha contenders. She doesn't pick fights, but when one is brought to her, she usually will answer with a snarl and a strong pounce. My friends call her "The Closer."

All three of my Labs love children. Cami is especially good with younger children, herding them and engaging them in play. A perfect babysitter, she keeps a watchful eye over them, keeping them out of mischief. Somehow the dogs know how to control themselves with the smaller children and do not knock them down or overwhelm them with attention.

They also love their people. Cami always stops by where you are sitting for "The Scratchings," wanting her head, ears, belly, and back scratched. She also brings over a toy to share or a ball to throw. She will bring her bone nearby, contentedly chewing on it so long as you are there. At night, she has taken over the bean bag chair for the winter months, and during the summer, she sleeps on the cool tiles of the bathroom floor. Competitive with Conner, she loves to chase a ball, stick, or even a Frisbee. When performing water retrieves, she plays a game where she brings the ball to the shore then somehow holds it under water with her forepaws, hiding it from the other dogs, and juggling it underwater to keep it submerged.

When they are not with me, they are with their "Granddad" on vacation in Pawley's Island, SC, or on Lake Toxaway, NC. All of my dogs like to watch TV, especially "Dog Whisperer" and Animal Planet shows. For some reason they love the movie *A River Runs Through It,* perhaps because I take them fly fishing. When things are working well, they stay downstream, inadvertently flushing the trout upstream for me.

Yes, they are spoiled. They eat high quality dog food, have baskets of toys, get kid's hamburgers at the drive-thru, ride in the car all the time, and a local butcher shop gives them free meat scraps on Fridays and Saturdays. They go to parks and the river, and are even invited to family gatherings.

Practically everyone who meets them loves them. My friend's young daughter would not sleep until her mom bought her a stuffed animal that looks just like Cami. She still sleeps with it every night. The dogs go individually to the nursing home to visit my two elderly relatives. The other residents also enjoy their visits. People who lay in a near-catatonic state, rouse themselves to pet the dogs, and it is magic to watch! The sitters and nurses, often from countries where dogs have a very different role in their culture, are usually frightened of the dogs at first. Time and again, these folks who are afraid of dogs find themselves actually petting them. The three dogs bring a lot of joy to many people. It seems that I am merely their chauffeur, chef, and program coordinator.

Giving Back

Camille, Conner, and Chip help me foster dogs and constitute a care-giving team, and they help immensely with foster dogs at our home. Some fosters do require some training, but most just need a calm and loving place to exist with people and other animals. They usually bloom back into their wonderful selves.

Rescue, adoption, and fostering are necessary, yet not sufficient. I lobby for an animal welfare legislation initiative, and I have drafted the Animal Welfare Reform Legislative Initiative for Georgia, addressing the source of all these pets in need of rescue: large numbers of people are not spaying and neutering their pets. I founded and continue to operate the SE Pet Rescue Railroad, SEPRR, which was originally created to facilitate the transport of animals from high-kill states to others who kill less. This allows people to learn about the movement, participate as drivers, cross-post transport run-sheets via email, and to get the word out on social media. The SEPRR has evolved to promote advocacy, spay-neuter, service dogs, and rescue-adoption organizations via social media. Simply put, SEPRR helps rescues by engaging a much larger audience than any one rescue could.

For hands on, nuts-and-bolts rescue work, I volunteer with Angels Among Us Pet Rescue, a non-profit volunteer-based organization dedicated to rescuing dogs and cats from high-kill shelters in north Georgia.

My passion stems from the love I have for my own dogs and the dogs I foster. Every time I look at them, I cannot escape the shattering thought of the thousands who did not get a home that are just like them–intelligent, loving, and creative. Adoption and rescue is so important and I hope I can make a difference by helping to save our wonderful companions.

- Bryan "Beau" Grant

Chancey

Chancey was approximately two years old when I adopted her from the Animal Hospital of Nicholasville, KY. My son's dog, Falco, a golden retriever, was living with me at the time. I had no plans to adopt another dog, however Chancey was so pathetic I knew no one would adopt her if I didn't bring her home.

I knew Chancey had special problems, but the vet at the clinic that rescued her really encouraged me and made it easy for me to bring her home. I've adopted all of my dogs except one in the past, so I was used to having dogs around.

By chance, Chancey came into my life. I actually went to the vet just to buy dog food. The vet technician was holding this pathetic, skinny, and badly injured little dog. I commented on how ugly she was, which I know was not a nice thing to say. I bought my dog food, got in my car and drove down the road for about five miles and turned back around. Two hours later she was sleeping on my queen-sized bed. Her name Chancey is short for "second chance," and I'm so glad the vet and I gave her one.

Chancey had been mauled by several large dogs, possibly part of the training for a fighting dog ring, when animal rescue brought her to the vet's office. The following Monday she was to be put to sleep because of her extensive injuries.   However, when Monday morning came, the vet decided to operate on her wounds. Her shoulder was so severely crushed that they weren't able to operate, but slowly she got better. She stayed at the clinic for nearly a month to heal before they started to look for a home for her. Now, after doubling her weight and some good grooming, she looks absolutely adorable!

She is a wonderful companion to me and sleeps on my bed next to my head. Falco and Chancey have become good friends, and even my daughter's dog, Molly, gets along with the pack. Chancey has learned to run again, as she could only walk on three legs when I got her. Two years later, she's running on all fours, but due to the injuries to her shoulder she can't run in a straight line, and her running is in a half circle.

Still a shy dog, on Halloween she shines. All three dogs get dressed in costume, and Chancey loves when the children come by for trick or treat. She greets them by excitedly wagging her tail. Last year she was dressed as a cow and loved every minute of it.

I knew some of what I was getting into by adopting a dog with a lot of emotional baggage and physical problems. Adoption is such a wonderful thing, but it's not something to be taken lightly, especially when adopting a dog like Chancey.

Chancey was very frightened when she came to live with me. She was afraid of people getting angry at her, and to this day I have to watch what I say to her. She is still emotionally fragile and I can't say "no" in a loud or frightening voice. She is more afraid of men, especially young men like those who had used her as bait. She's slowly learning and becoming more comfortable, and I've learned how much discipline she can tolerate. I'm fortunate that she is so well behaved that I don't need to discipline her too much. She sticks to me like Velcro, and considering all she's been through, that's just fine with me.

- Carol Damen

Declan and Shiner

Declan and Shiner were two years old when we adopted them, three years apart, from an animal rescue group. We had an Aussie for over 12 years before Declan and Shiner came into our lives.

Our first Australian shepherd, Idgie, came to us as a seemingly abandoned puppy. It took us a while to agree to take her in because Dru had real hesitations about getting a dog without a tail. After all, how could she communicate with us? Idgie was extremely smart and totally devoted to us, but she was not keen on a lot of other people or animals. We really couldn't take her out with us off leash, but we adored her and she solidified our love for Aussies. After she passed away it took us a couple of years to decide on getting another, but we were certain we wanted another Aussie. When we were ready to have another dog in our lives, we never really thought of getting a dog any other way than through some form of adoption. There are so many pets in shelters that need a home.

First came Declan

We started looking on a rescue website for a while prior to adopting. We were very familiar with Aussies and their varying levels of need for activity. We were looking for a "low energy" Aussie who would like a lot of activity and walks, but not in constant need of having a job to do or have any obsessive behaviors.

At first, we were looking to adopt a female. We saw a very small red merle female Aussie on the website. While small, she seemed packed with personality and a good fit for us. After getting approved to adopt we learned she had been approved for adoption with another family. We were pleased for her and continued combing the nearby states' website pages. The woman who performed our in-home interview asked us if we had ever considered adopting a male. She continued, saying that although males are often a little slower to learn new commands, when they learn they "have it," and they tend to respond very well to female humans.

Concurrently, we noted Declan on the North Carolina/ South Carolina rescue website. He was approximately two years old, got along with cats (we had an elderly cat at that time), was described as low energy, and he was a beautiful red merle, which is what we had our sights set on. We wrote the appropriate contact and expressed sincere interest. He was being fostered in Apex, NC. We were going out of the country for holiday a few days later and we didn't want to pass up the opportunity to be in line to adopt him, so we drove to Apex and met with the foster parents, their two Aussies, and Declan. At first, he was a bit shy and reticent, but he was very amenable to letting us pet him and take him for a walk. It was apparent that he was gentle and easy going. He seemed a bit worn, and there was a sense of calmness yet loneliness in his eyes.

He seemed to trust us and connect, and we felt that we could grow well together. So all was put in motion to take him home with us once we got home from vacation. The rescue group transported Declan to Charlotte where we could easily pick him up after flying in from vacation. As it turned out, his temporary home belonged to the lady who originally pulled Declan out of the kill shelter in Fort Mill, SC. She was also the one who named him Declan, from the Irish Saint Declan, meaning "man of peace and prayer." Perfect!

Declan immediately took to Linda. It was almost unhealthy the way he needed her. It seemed that he saw in her his special person from his previous life. Whoever that was, it was someone special, and they obviously spent a lot of time with him. He came to us already knowing multiple commands–sit, shake, beg, dance, and even how to perfectly walk on a leash and heel. He stayed right with us on walks and it was clear he did not need a leash. His ability to respond to voice command was amazing.

Declan seemed rather depressed for several months after our adoption. It seemed clear that he appreciated us and was comfortable in his new home, however we had the feeling that it was hard for him to shake certain thoughts of his past life. He was afraid of our TV remote and of the clicking on our grill starter. One night we think we figured out the origin of those fears. A friend of ours who had just joined the "XXX" was at our house and pulled out her new pistol. When she popped out the magazine, Declan, who was not in sight of the gun, took off and was uneasy for a few days. We now think his fear of the remote was really a fear of guns and that he must have been shot at during his life on his own. We are very pleased that he is no longer afraid of the remote, yet he still makes himself scarce when it's time to grill because the click of the automatic ignition mechanism brings back a bad memory.

After a while, Declan seemed to pull out of his depression and embrace his new life. He loves to do tricks and run in open fields and play with other dogs. It seemed that he would continue to grow and benefit from a full-time playmate who spoke his particular language. Plus, we noticed that individually we were starting to peruse the rescue website pages and talk about other Aussies out there who needed a home.

Welcome Shiner

While looking for a sibling for Declan, we thought that another male would be good, and definitely another lower energy boy with an easy disposition. We read about Maxx, a heartworm-positive blue merle found in Raleigh, NC, who was being fostered and nursed back to health in Georgia. We read his description and instantly fell for him. But there was one problem–he had a tail! We had not had a dog with a tail in years, and while there are different thoughts about whether to crop or not crop a dog's tail, we had gotten used to having dogs without a tail. Aussies are widely known as "wiggle butts." It's almost like their bodies are segmented. Their whole bodies wiggle in different directions. During all of this wiggling, the lack of a tail proves safe for anything in tail reach–coffee, wine, items on tables, etc.

We began communicating via email with Maxx's foster mom. She further enlightened us about him, and we shared more about Declan and our life. Maxx was being fostered in a home dedicated to care for dogs with heartworms. Other families expressed interest in adopting Maxx, but we stayed on that list and kept in communication with his foster parents. We developed a genuine care for his parents, and through them we developed a love for Maxx.

Maxx was medically cleared and ready for his forever

home near the time we were heading to Hilton Head Island, SC. His foster home was two hours south and all was cleared for his foster parents to bring him to Hilton Head Island, meet us, and determine if all was a good fit. It was very important to his foster parents for him to never think that we took him from his home, rather he left his home to go to another. This spoke volumes to us.

On meeting day, the foster parents with their two Aussies and Maxx drove into the parking lot. Instead of being overwhelmed, Declan and Maxx instinctively went to each other as if no other dogs were around. It was as if they knew they were to be connected.

Maxx didn't seem to be attached to or relate to his name, so we renamed him. After a bit of thought, Dru looked at him and said, "Shiner." It's a perfect name for him, since a marking over one eye makes it appear as if he has a permanent "black eye."

Shiner is a lover. He loves everyone and loves to nuzzle. He, too, has an aversion to clicks, including the sound of a finger nail clipper and a camera shutter. When he hears such a sound, he quickly, yet quietly, leaves the room and seeks shelter away from whatever sound caused him trauma in his previous life.

Shiner has a very well-developed sense of smell and is led by his nose. One evening he bounded from the yard like a flash. We saw a fawn scamper through a neighboring yard. Then, Shiner came sprinting through the woods with a doe close on his heels. Shiner came back home 40 minutes later, obviously beat, worn out, but not bloody. While we have been told that Aussies do not do well with invisible fences, we decided to invest in one. It has worked out well. It is as if this "invisible boundary" gave Shiner a sense of place and even comfort. The boys are doing great and have learned to play together even more since Shiner knows his boundaries. He is now staying with his humans and brother without a leash on walks in our neighborhood and on the beach, is coming well when called, and is readily learning new commands. They have learned to share very well, and they engage in multiple daily lick fests –licking each others' eyes and mouths. One adopted Aussie is great; two adopted Aussies are even greater.

- Linda Robinson and Dru Henson

Declan and Shiner

Photo by Yvonne Flowers

Dottie

Dottie, a female rat terrier/pointer mix, was five months old when we adopted her. A friend associated with a local humane society found her rummaging through a dumpster on a construction site and took her in. Email blasts were sent to personal contacts about the availability of the little black-and-white girl, and we decided to go and meet her. Dottie adopted us the moment Susan sat on the floor, and Dottie snuggled in her lap.

Dottie was our first adoption as a couple. We are grateful to our friend who made it so easy for Dottie to come to live with us.

Dottie is the most persistent, diplomatic dog we have ever seen. When we first got her, we had an older cat. Since Dottie is a bit high strung, we kept them separated. It started with a plywood pen in the garage (four feet high), which Dottie eventually jumped. We then tried to keep Dottie on the lower level of our two-story home, which worked until she figured out how to creep up the stairs softly enough to not rattle her collar. Now our cat is in heaven, and Dottie is in our bed.

Dottie's Quirks

She is not a fan of water, but will jump in the tub for bathing and back out when finished with a spurt of energy only a lightning bolt could match. She is a natural hunter, whose to-date prey count includes six squirrels, a large rabbit, three moles, and a lizard. In just five minutes, she has the ability to woo anyone—even those who will try to avoid her – to see her point of view. She is incredibly intelligent, full of personality, and undyingly loving and loyal – all qualities of a great dog.

- Steve and Susan Crain

Photo by Yvonne Flowers

Duke, Parker and Spirit

Duke

My Labrador retriever, Duke, was a puppy when he came into my life and was two years old when I adopted him. At the time of adoption I was raising a guide dog puppy for Southeastern Guide Dogs in Palmetto, FL.

Duke is a "career change" dog from Southeastern Guide Dogs, who continued to work as a gifted canine. I wanted a dog to help me with raising future guide dog puppies. No doubt, it is much easier when the puppies have an adult dog as their model. Duke was my first adopted dog, and I recently have adopted another Southeastern puppy named Parker. Together we are currently raising a new puppy, Spirit. It just would not feel right if there were not plenty of dogs in the house!

I was acquainted with Duke prior to his adoption and was thrilled with the opportunity to have him become part of our family. Duke was raised at Ridgeland Correctional Institution, Ridgeland, SC, as part of Southeastern's Inmates

Providing Animal Care and Training (IMPACT) program. I was Duke's weekend parent when he was a puppy. My volunteer duties were to provide maximum socialization and exposure to new situations and people, as well as work on in-home manners. Because I was involved in the program at Ridgeland, when it was decided that Duke would change careers, the school gave me the unique opportunity to adopt Duke, even though I was not his full-time raiser.

Duke's claim to fame is that he was part of the cast of Animal Planet's *Cell Dogs* series, filmed while he was a puppy at Ridgeland. Since his adoption, Duke has been tested and registered with The Delta Society's Pet Partners and Therapy Dogs International (TDI). He also is recognized as an AKC Canine Good Citizen. In addition to his regular visits to nursing homes and hospice patients as a TDI ambassador, Duke has been on countless outings and to group functions and speaking engagements with our puppies on behalf of Southeastern.

Career-change dogs can have many career paths as gifted canines. Some will serve as bomb-sniffing or arson dogs, assistance dogs for disabled persons, and sometimes as companions for soldiers returning home from war. Recently, Southeastern – through "Paws for Patriots" – has placed therapy dogs at Walter Reed Medical Center and at the Bethesda National Naval Hospital. They are also placing companion service dogs with returning soldiers suffering from the effects of post-traumatic stress syndrome.

Now more than eight years old, Duke hasn't retired and is still an all-around great working dog. He is wonderful with children, as well as with elderly adults, and although he did not become a guide dog, I truly believe he has provided an invaluable service to many as a therapy dog. Best of all, he loves his work and is truly gifted.

- Susan Souder

Frida

We adopted Frida from the rescue organization Chihuahua Rescue USA, which rescues dogs from the eastern and central United States including the Carolinas, Kentucky, Indiana, and Michigan.

She was approximately one-and-a-half-years-old at the time. She is a Chihuahua/rat terrier mix; such mixes are commonly called miniature rat terriers, but Frida may have more Chihuahua in her than they commonly do.

I had always wanted a Chihuahua, although I knew very little about the breed. I knew they were small, sassy and bonded strongly with their owners. In addition, we wanted a small dog because we already had two pets and live in a smaller home. I knew I needed help in choosing a dog, and I knew I did not want to buy a dog from a pet store because of the connection to puppy mills. When I contacted Chihuahua Rescue, it became personal right from the start. They asked me a lot of questions about our lifestyle and what personality of dog would fit best for our family. I knew it was the right choice then to work with this rescue organization to find our dog.

It was a very smooth process, especially since it was our first adoption experience. I first filled out a questionnaire on the website, where they had the available dogs listed along with descriptions of each dog's background and personality provided by the foster families they live with until they are adopted. The questionnaire was phrased in a way that allowed me to express my personality and talk about my family and how we hoped our dog would fit into it. I looked through the available dogs' profiles and tried to choose a couple I thought would work with our family. A representative from the rescue then contacted me personally and we kept in touch for the next two weeks by email and phone while we searched for and found our dog.

The representative looked through the dogs I selected through the website and compared my questionnaire application to the dogs' personalities. It turned out the ones I chose were not as compatible as I had thought, but she had just rescued two dogs from a shelter who had come from a hoarder home. They were both female, and both had litters of puppies. Between them they had nine puppies. All the puppies were adopted from the shelter and the mommas were left behind and would have been euthanized. A worker at the shelter contacted Chihuahua Rescue to see if they could take the dogs, and one of the dogs seemed like she would be a perfect fit for my family. They sent me pictures and described her personality, and I knew this was the dog for us.

After we found her, we arranged a meeting place and I picked her up and brought her home. There was an adoption fee, and I could not have felt better paying it, because it was going directly to another rescue dog needing surgery after being hit by a car. They had also spayed my dog and gave her the first round of shots, and I got all of her records from the shelter and the rescue organization. In all, she was not in foster care long before she came to our house.

We will always adopt or rescue animals. We would never buy one from a breeder or a pet store knowing that there are so many amazing dogs out there that need homes. Even though this was our first formal adoption, I have rescued several animals, including three stray cats and a rabbit, and fostered them until I could find them homes. We keep in touch with some of the families of our rescues so we get updates on how they are doing. There is nothing better than knowing you helped a suffering animal find happiness and safety to live out the rest of their time here on this earth.

Funny, she doesn't look like a Susan

We renamed our girl Frida; initially the rescue group had named her Susan. My husband was traveling for work, so a friend went with me to pick her up. When my girlfriend and I were driving home with her, we decided she did not look like a Susan at all. I'm an art teacher, and there are lots of women artists who are my heroes, one of whom is Frida Khalo. Given all that Susan had been through in her life, and the fact that she is a Chihuahua mix with a Mexican heritage of sorts, I decided Frida was the most fitting name.

Frida was so scared once we adopted her. I'm sure with everything she had been through in such a short period of time, she did not know what to think about what was happening to her. But they put her in my arms and I just felt like I could make her happy. I wanted nothing more than to protect and heal her, and earn her trust so that she could be happy. When we got her home to meet her two siblings (our two cats) she just slept and slept. During the first week I had her I was alone with a hectic work schedule. I regret not being able to take some days off right after I adopted her, just so I could have helped her more with the transition. We had some rough patches those first few days, but we were soon into a routine and she began to come out of her shell. We are still seeing parts of her personality continue to emerge as the years go by.

She is very attached to me. She loves my husband, but there is something to be said about Chihuahuas being one-person dogs. She loves walks, and we can walk for an hour or more and she will still be raring to go. She is a bit of a princess, as she won't walk if the sidewalk is wet, or if it's too hot or too windy. She won't walk in the winter at all.

Frida loves chasing squirrels, but has only played a proper game of fetch with a ball once or twice. Instead, she has furry little rodent toys and we play "get-it" where she practices pursuit and capture. She hates water and swimming. She loves basking in the sun. Even when she's been indoors for eight hours, when I take her outside to go to the bathroom on a sunny day she will just park herself on the grass to soak up some rays and put off doing her business until later.

She sleeps with us at night and is a total burrower. She will go under the covers all the way to our feet and sleep there all night. Or she will end up between our pillows. She found her bark a long time after we got her, and we didn't even know she could bark! Now she barks at the cats, at passing dogs and at approaching strangers. She's turning into a good little guard dog. Even though she loves walks, she hates her harness and leash. She will roll onto her back and look up at me with pleading eyes, as if to say, "Mom, don't make me wear that thing again!" When we visit my in-laws, she can run free in the woods and she goes nuts, running around like crazy for hours. It's her favorite place, with lots of squirrels and no leash.

- Erin Ledyard

Georgia

We already had two dogs when we found Georgia—Chloe Jean, a Yorkshire terrier, and Madigan Rae (Maddie), a border collie. Georgia, a purebred golden retriever, was just 13- months-old when we found her in a shelter in Dallas, TX. This was the same rescue where we had found Georgia's soon-to-be best friend, Maddie, several months earlier. The folks at the shelter provided as much information as possible on both Georgia's and Maddie's histories and patiently answered our questions.

We weren't fans of her name, but it seemed to fit her personality somehow, so we kept it. Fast forward to six years later and we are now living in the state of Georgia. My husband likes to joke that if she had been named Hawaii we'd be living there now. Perhaps during our next rescue adventure we'll take more interest in the name of the dog we select!

I've often heard people say you don't always select the

dog, the dog selects you. This was never more true than with Georgia Kaye. My husband happened to be having lunch down the road from the shelter one day and found himself with a few extra minutes on his lunch hour. So he stopped in to see the dogs. As he walked by her pen, Georgia reached out and grabbed his leg with her paw, so he stopped. We were fairly new pet parents and didn't really know anything about golden retrievers or have a particular fondness or devotion for any breed.

The next thing I knew, I was paged at work for an urgent phone call. In those days, my husband worked in the laboratory of a chemical plant so my mind leaped and my heart raced fearing the worst as I took the call. The "urgency" turned out to be that my husband wanted to bring this "little" girl home with him and was looking for my blessing. All I could say was, "aren't goldens really big dogs?" and "we have two dogs already, I think that's more than enough!" His reply was, "she's not THAT big and her days are numbered here." What he neglected to share with me was that she had been returned twice for behavior problems. That, coupled with her size and age, made her less desirable. And so our life with one very special golden retriever named Georgia Kaye began.

A few weeks after adopting our Golden Girl, my husband and I had reason to leave the house for a couple of hours. When I returned, she had completely trashed our house. There was no doubt which dog did the dirty work! Our Yorkie was six pounds and our border collie was doing the best she could to be invisible. Georgia had destroyed a six-foot palm tree that was sitting in the living room front window. She chewed the plastic pot to bits and in the process shredded the tree and laced the living room walls, carpet and stairs with mud. There was mud all over the entire first floor of our house. I tried to put this 70 pound dog in a crate but she would have no part of it. All four legs went in different directions as she tried to show me who was boss. I did, however, win that battle of wills as she tested the limits of my patience.

From that day forward, Georgia was absolutely perfect. She never did another thing wrong, ever. It was as if she said "thanks for not kicking me to the curb like the other two families did. I'll straighten up and fly right now." She is calm, patient, loving, and obedient, following every command to the letter.

One night, however, Georgia and Maddie joined forces. The herding instinct in Maddie took over and the retriever in Georgia surfaced. During a 3:00 a.m. potty break they cornered a rabbit, brought it into the house and, much to my sleeping husband's chagrin, laid it on his chest. The story has a happy ending because I believe that at the time of this writing the rabbit is living out his golden years in the Lone Star state.

Georgia does have her quirks. She has a yellow lacrosse ball that is her security blanket and without it she is lost. But the one quirk that stands out most is her propensity to be a tattletale. Throughout the eight years that Georgia has been part of our family, we have adopted, and sadly lost, several dogs. We lost both our Yorkie and Georgia's best friend and soul sister, Maddie, tragically in 2005. Poor Georgia had no idea how to be an only dog, so we took her to a shelter to pick out a new buddy. After parading a litany of dogs in various ages, sizes, colors, and sexes in front of her she picked an eight-week-old male mutt. This was our first experience with puppies and we made a few mistakes in the process of raising him. Whenever anything was wrong, big sister Georgia would come shaking from top to tail and find my husband or me. She relentlessly whined and nudged us until we got the message to follow her to the scene of the crime. To this day, five years and three dogs later, she is still the world's biggest tattletale.

Throughout the 20 years that I've had dogs as a loving part of my family, I have never witnessed a dog grieve the way this girl did when that puppy passed away. Baxter, our shelter mutt, died at 26 months from leukemia, after just three days of showing symptoms. When I came home from the animal hospital Georgia met me at the door. I looked at her, sobbed, and said "he's gone baby." Somehow she seemed to understand completely and I witnessed something I have never before seen. She ran up and down the stairs of our house searching every room wailing at the top of her lungs like a wounded animal. To me, Baxter was what I lovingly referred to as my soul dog. I think to Georgia Kaye it was like losing a child. She had basically raised him, teaching him everything from eight weeks old to 26 months. I think she grieved as deeply as I did.

Full House

The Internet has now made it much easier to find your perfect "fur kid" online. We will always adopt or rescue dogs. In fact, after adopting Georgia, we adopted not only Baxter from a shelter in upstate New York, we also adopted a schnoodle (Sophie Ann) from a shelter in Connecticut, a shih tzu (Toby Austin) from a shelter in Suwanee, GA, and most recently a golden retriever/German shepherd mix (Cassiopeia Rae) from a shelter in Winder, GA. Our family is not perfect by any definition, but the amount of unconditional love we give and receive is astounding. Shelter animals sometimes come with baggage and their share of emotional and physical scars, but when you work through the issues with them the experience is incredibly rewarding. These animals seem to spend their life appreciating every scent, sound and dog biscuit to the ultimate degree. In other words, they realize they've received a second chance at life.

I enjoy volunteering with many pet organizations. I

volunteered for the Georgia SPCA for a brief time after moving to Georgia; that's how I came home with a shih tzu and finally decided I needed to channel my energy elsewhere. I currently volunteer for the pet food bank, Daffy's Pet Soup Kitchen, and serve on the board of an animal welfare organization, Sunbear Squad. The most rewarding of all my volunteer activities is the pet therapy visits I perform with Georgia Kaye. With other team members we visit assisted living facilities and schools for mentally and physically handicapped children on a weekly basis. In addition, we perform special visits on occasion. We've been to a battered women's shelter, hospitals, and this summer we were part of a team visiting a bereavement camp, bringing joy to children dealing with the recent loss of a loved one.

Georgia may have had a bit of a rough start, being adopted out and returned to the shelter twice only to be put on the short list, but she must have recognized a golden opportunity when she saw my husband and reached out to him. He turned out to be her ticket to the good life she's living now. In fact, not only did we settle in "her" state, we bought a home with a beautiful in-ground pool where she swims every day to benefit her senior hips and joints.

I encourage everyone to search the shelters and rescue organizations when it is time to add a new fur kid to the family. They will be thankful for the new lease on life and will be a continual blessing.

- Christy Morrison

Gracie

We got 12-week-old Gracie, a Boston terrier mix, on Memorial Day weekend at a shelter in Greenville, SC. At the time we had one other dog, a sheltie named Chaos, who was seven years old. Chaos had been a backyard breeder dog. I didn't know what that was – I just knew he needed out of that situation.

Gracie found her way into our hearts by accident. I had been looking online at dogs, but wasn't very serious about it. That day, a friend and I were headed to the farmers market, but they were closed. Instead we went to TJ Maxx and somehow ended up at the shelter, which was just up the street. I had never adopted a dog or even stepped foot inside a shelter.

If I was to get another dog, I actually thought about getting a Chihuahua. The day we were at the shelter, none of the dogs jumped out at me, so we wandered to the puppy room. I was playing with a tiny puppy, then looked up at his roommate–and there was Gracie, shaking like a leaf with the biggest "Flying Nun" ears I've ever seen. I pulled her out, and we went into a room. I had no intentions of adopting her, so I held her a little and put her back to go look at an adult Chihuahua I had seen earlier. I took the Chihuahua out and tried to interact with him, but he could not have cared less about me. I went and pulled Gracie back out and she put her paws around my neck–and that was it; she was leaving with me, done deal.

Gracie is very particular with the dogs she plays with and likes. She has an odd and somewhat scary habit of sticking her head inside larger dogs' mouths, and I'm not sure what that's all about. She's a terrier, though, so that explains some of it!

Adopting Gracie was just the beginning. I now volunteer with the intake facility in Greenville, which is where the dogs at risk of being euthanized are held, and I started rescuing dogs not long after adopting Gracie. There are so many great rescue organizations, but I wanted to do something different. My husband and I discussed different ideas, but we kept coming back to senior dogs. We did some research and realized that there are less than 10 rescue organizations in the United States that focus solely on senior dogs, and only one that we could find in our area. We also were amazed and saddened at how many senior dogs are in shelters. The shelters can be very stressful and disorienting for them. Sadly, they have little to no chance of adoption and many are not even given the opportunity. That sealed it for us. Classic Canine was born.

Classic Canine's home base is located in McCormick, SC. Triple Oak Ranch, home of Classic Canine, is a hobby farm where we have set up a wonderful, stimulating environment for the retirees that reside there. The animals have a huge play yard to roam and supervise us while we are working. We have learned these old kids take this seriously.

We had no idea how much supervision and help we needed! The more we have gotten to know and work with senior dogs, the more we love them. They are so much fun and have big personalities. We believe that every senior dog deserves a warm bed and lots of love.

- Jennifer Wilke

Heidi

When I saw Heidi, I thought she was an older dog due to her broken teeth, and I adopted her to be a companion to my older collie, Prince. I found out later how wrong I was. She is a husky mix and full of energy.

Heidi was brought in to the veterinary clinic where I work by the animal shelter for a lump on her shoulder. I happened to glance into the room where she was being examined and immediately was drawn to her. She was so happy and smiled at me. I couldn't resist.

Heidi was a stray the shelter picked up and no one ever claimed. I learned quickly that Heidi is a dominant female. She dominates through minor nuances that other dogs immediately understand. She quietly establishes her authority with other dogs. We often go on walks and she will position herself between me and any other dog if she is concerned about that dog's intentions. We have had many people bring their dogs here to take walks, as we live in the country, and Heidi is never aggressive, knowing they are no threat. She is extremely intelligent and benevolent, but is definitely the boss. She has chased away many trespassing critters such as raccoons, possums, and especially coyotes. Of all of my adopted pets, Heidi is the most challenging because of her free spirit.

Her bad teeth were due to chewing on a chain or chain-link fence. I have a box full of collars, halters and gentle leaders, and she can slip all of them, even on walks. She is a true husky at heart. She, much to my horror, was like the dog in the movie *Funny Farm*. I would catch glimpses of her running in the distance with no hope of catching her. I reclaimed her from two different shelters after she was apprehended. I was always happy to pay the fees. Several times she made it to the closest town and went to the local convenience store. They would call me and I would drive there only to see her loose, watching the cars go by and she would come running when I pulled up. I had many sleepless hours worrying about Heidi being lost and in danger. I was very lucky. Eventually she became good friends with the neighbor dog down the road and they split their time between my house and that house. Now that she is older she likes to stay at home and be a couch potato.

All of my adopted pets have come from the local shelter. In adopting an older dog, most people will get one which is already housebroken and is mature enough to realize they are loved and wanted. The dog can appreciate a good home after not having one, and I truly think they can differentiate a shelter from a home.

I adopt dogs and cats because they need a home and I can give them a good one. I believe this is the best way to get a pet. The one exception I have made was a sheltie puppy with a bad heart. The owners knew they could not sell her and said that they would give her to me if I promised to give her the medical care she would need. After an expensive heart surgery, I'm happy to report she is a happy, healthy three-year-old and fits in well with the rest of the family.

- Patty Amsrud

Hemingway

Hemingway, once known by his racing name of Iruska Hemi, is a retired racing greyhound, and he was three and one-half years old when he came into my life. When Hemingway came to live with us we had three cats, including two rescues. We adopted Hemingway from Greyhound Pets of America, Richmond, Virginia chapter (now known as James River Greyhounds). While I have rescued and adopted pets all of my life (which has included stopping on interstates and picking up turtles trying to cross the road) this experience was different because I was responding to a recently discovered passion for this particular breed.

I discovered greyhounds when I was passing through PetSmart one day. A greyhound adoption group was there with their rescue dogs, and the instant that I saw one of these beautiful, elegant, and gentle creatures, I felt an intense connection to and longing for a greyhound of my own. Call it chemistry, fate, or serendipity, but the first time I looked into the soulful eyes of a greyhound, I knew that not only would I have one in my life, but that our journey together would change my life, which it did. I always prefer to say that I did not rescue them, but they rescued me.

The adoption process with Hemingway was unique to any other adoption experience, as my greyhound was delivered to Virginia from Florida by a pre-arranged event called a "dog haul." Hemingway came to Virginia from Jefferson County Kennel Club, a racetrack located in Monticello, FL, along with 13 other greyhounds. They all travel together in separate crates in a truck. Making the long journey along the East coast is a very stressful event for them. Once they come off the truck, one by one, they receive a small meal, a warm bath, ear cleaning, nail trimming, and their first hug from their forever home adopter. It's a little different than picking up a new puppy in a breeder's home or visiting a pet shelter. The experience was quite awesome, watching them take their first steps off the race track and into my heart.

Meant to Be

When I completed the adoption application for a greyhound, I specified that I wanted one that would make a good therapy dog, able to visit patients in hospitals, nursing homes, and hospice. I requested a female, and I had hoped for a white dog with tan spots. The greyhound adoption group notified me that they had just the dog for me, so all was going as planned. However, closer to the dog haul day when we would meet our dogs, I received an email from the adoption counselor that was in charge of the greyhound placement in Florida. She had actually pulled a dog away from someone else to give him to me, because she thought he had the perfect qualities for a therapy dog. In greyhound terms, it is called being "wiggly," which means the dog is very expressive and somewhat wiggles when he walks, almost like being an extrovert and nerd at the same time! So, I ended up with a fawn-colored male, completely different from what I had requested. But the moment I saw him, I knew he and I were going to have a remarkable life together. Iruska Hemi became Hemingway that day, and he ran his last race, right into my heart. Although I did not pick him, I believe he was picked for me and was destined to be with me. I cannot imagine my life without him now.

I believe each dog has his or her own unique personality traits or characteristics that endear him or her to us in some special way. I see the way Hemingway interacts with others, and they see his gentleness, sweetness, expressive eyes, and his outgoing personality. He is very intelligent and responsive to my actions and words. I have to spell "walk" and "treat," because if I say those words, he will even wake from a deep sleep to respond to them. When I only give him one treat, he is relentless in pursuing me until he gets his second treat. He is so smart that he can count! Even at night, when he is sleeping soundly in his bed in the den, and I leave the den to go to sleep, within minutes Hemingway sashays into the bedroom and plops down on his other bed, which is located next to mine. I may think he's in a deep sleep, but I know he's always listening to my every move and word. Even when I take his food bowl to its stand across the kitchen, he nudges me with his long nose all the way there, as if to say, "I've been waiting for this all day; hurry up!"

Hemingway is a Delta Society-certified therapy dog, and he has just the perfect personality to make someone's bad day a little brighter. I am currently working to get his Therapy Dog International certification, along with participating in Hos-Pets, a local organization that brings therapy dogs and hospice patients together to create miracles through communication, companionship, and comfort.

Within six months of having Hemingway, we adopted a second greyhound named Isabella, who had the racing name As the Bell Tolls, and she has now received her Therapy Dog International certification so that she can join Hemingway in visiting patients in hospitals, nursing homes, and hospice. Greyhounds make wonderful therapy dogs. If all the economic and situational stars were aligned perfectly, I would have hundreds of greyhounds living happily ever after with me!

When one adopts a retired racing greyhound, the racing statistics for the last season are provided to the adopter. I was curious, so I compared Isabella's racing earnings to Hemingway's. Isabella earned $1,898 for the season, while Hemingway only earned $18.36! I know why, too. I can only imagine that once that race gate opened, Hemingway must have seen the crowd of people in the stands and wanted to meet each and every one of them. I believe the real reason he was such a lousy racer was that he was smart enough to learn how to lose, because he knew there was a better life out there for him. Hemingway has taught me that it's okay to lose the race, because the real prize isn't always the money.

My love for greyhounds did not stop with adopting them. I volunteered with the organization from where I adopted Hemingway and served on its board of directors until my relocation to Hilton Head Island, SC. Once on Hilton Head Island, I joined a greyhound adoption group named Savannah Friends of Greyhounds as Pets, where I currently serve on the board of directors.

One very special thing about dogs, I have learned, is that they live in the present. For example, if I leave the house for five minutes or for five hours, their greeting at the door for me has the same level of excitement, and they wag their tails and shake their heads up and down in a frenzy, as if to say, "You're back! Why did you take so long?" The food I put in their bowls each morning and evening is the same food they've been getting for months and months, but when I serve it to them, they are just as excited as if they were being served filet mignon. They don't dwell on the past or have angst about the future. They live in the present. I continue to learn from Hemingway and Isabella, and I thank them for rescuing me.

- Karen Shea

Hemingway and Isabella

Spots, Hogan and Jackson

Hogan and Pack

My passion for rescue dogs started with Hogan. Hogan was found by a woman in Ridgeland, SC, who brought him to our kennel. A black Labrador, Dalmation, and great Dane mix, he was only nine weeks old, and I had no choice but to take him home with me while I looked for a more permanent home. At first, I nearly had to choose between my husband and this puppy, but a couple of days later, my husband had fallen in love with him, too.

Hogan has always been skittish, and at first I didn't trust him with children. I taught our children how to be gentle with animals and to always ask me before petting them. Now Hogan is the boys' dear friend and always licks their boo-boos when they get hurt.

After Hogan came Raynie, Toby, Bella, and Spots–all from Jasper Animal Rescue Mission in Ridgeland. Raynie was a badly abused petite black and tan rottweiler mix. She was six months old and quickly became my project. She was so scared, but little by little I gained her trust. It was more than a year before she would let others pet her. She is still a little shy and has become my office dog at the kennel.

I got Toby when I sent one of my employees to Jasper for puppies. They brought back several puppies, which were all adopted out, but we decided to keep Toby. He was a white-and-tan bulldog mix with a bad limp. We learned the limp in his back leg was neurological and that he was in no pain. We took him to a chiropractor and a holistic veterinarian, wanting to try everything to help him. He still doesn't have much use of both hind legs and hops around like a bunny. Toby has turned out to be a great dog and loves our boys. He is also an office dog and stays at the kennel.

Next came Bella, an Italian greyhound/Chihuahua mix. She was in a pen with other puppies who beat her up. We brought her home for the night and she stayed.

Spots is a great Dane mix. She was first named Filet because she looked like the Chick-Fil-A cow. My husband has a fondness for black-and-white puppies, so you know we had to keep her, too. She was found in a Tupperware container when she was two days old. We bottle fed her and she now weighs in at 80 pounds. Her favorite thing to do is to cuddle on the sofa under the blanket in between the kids while watching cartoons.

Jackson, a yellow Labrador retriever, came from an animal control center in Georgia. We brought several puppies home from there who were ill, including Jackson. We put them in our mudroom, gave them antibiotics and de-worming medication, and nursed them back to health. And yes, Jackson stayed with us, too.

Our latest rescue dog is Baylor, a stray black-and-tan yard dog who came running up to me at a grocery store in Bluffton, SC. He was probably three or four years old at the time, and of course I had to bring him home, too.

With all of the dogs I encounter who desperately need

homes, I thought I should start my own shelter, attached to my boarding kennel, Brooke's Bed & Biscuit in Bluffton, SC. Brooke's Haven Animal Rescue was born, and now my passion for finding loving homes for rescue animals has an actual structure. Each dog or cat we bring in we take to the vet and give heartworm treatment as needed. We have designated 800 square feet at the kennel for these homeless dogs. We average 15 dogs at a time. Most of our rescues are adopted by clients, family, and friends. It's very exciting to see our rescue dogs, who were once skinny, flea-infested, and afraid, come back healthy and happy to board at our kennel.

Of course, this all comes at a cost. For every animal I bring home, my husband gets a new toy, including a Jeep and two four-wheelers. I guess that's a fair trade!

- Brooke Fisher

Baylor

Jack

Jackson, or Jack for short, was just two months old when I adopted him. I found him on Petfinder.com and rescued him from Mary Ann Morris Animal Society, Inc. (MAMAS Shelter) in Bamberg, SC. Jack is my first dog on my own and I thought it was such a great concept to adopt a dog. We had pure bred golden retrievers growing up, so I was fond of that breed, and I wanted to give a home to a dog that needed one.

I saw from the photograph on Petfinder.com that Jack had blonde, thick Elizabeth Taylor eye lashes that made me fall in love with him. When I drove the three hours to get him, it was the biggest step off a cliff I had ever taken. It had been years since I had a dog and my parents were there then to help me raise them. I'm so glad I did this as it has been the best experience I have ever been through and has changed the direction of my life. I believe that experiences pick you and this one had my name all over it.

A Ruff Beginning

At just six months old Jack started showing serious signs of slowing down. After consulting with my vet, he recommended seeing a surgeon. We found out he needed a triple pelvic osteotomy, which means in general terms a three-part hip replacement in both hips. The surgery was going to cost over $5,000, which was something I definitely didn't have.

The dog community on Hilton Head Island, led by a wonderful friend, Beth, came together and raised the money needed for Jack's surgery. What I found out going through this experience was that it wasn't about the love I had for Jack, it was the fact that I didn't have the money to save him alone, and I am not the only person who has gone through this experience.

The experience changed my life forever and I wanted to come up with a way to help other families who find themselves in similar situations with their rescue pets. And so the company, Ruff Life, was born. Ruff Life is a line of products including t-shirts, sweat shirts, dog collars, and toys, and the inventory continues to expand. The original artwork represents the rescue animals that we save. Profits go toward helping families who need financial assistance with their rescue dog's medical bills. Any money left over will be donated to local animal shelters.

Jack has turned out to be a healthy, happy dog. I call him little Jerry Seinfeld because he is hilarious. He is a "butt man" and likes to bite all my female friends and family on the — well, you guessed it. He always gets you when you least expect it.

I also rescued and fostered another dog who was adopted by a family, but it didn't work out. She is now placed with friends of mine and we get to see her every day on the beach. I also volunteer with the Hilton Head Humane Association.

I feel I will always help rescue dogs and will always adopt. I would never go another way!

- Julie Nickerson

Leroy and TJ

Leroy Brown was just six months old when I saw him. He's a border collie mix, and I adopted him from the Kentucky Humane Society. It was five years later that I adopted one-year-old TJ from my cousin. TJ is also a border collie mix, and loves his big brother, Leroy.

I wanted to rescue dogs because they usually turn out to be so smart and so grateful. I would rather save one from being euthanized than go out and spend a ridiculous amount of money on a purebred. Both adoption experiences were good, and I had adopted a dog once before, so I wasn't new to the process. I would absolutely do it again.

Emotionally for me, getting Leroy was tough. I had adopted a pound puppy before that didn't work out. It was a really sad situation, because she was extremely aggressive, and after much work and training, I had to give her up. My heart was so broken, but when I got settled in Kentucky I was ready for another dog, or so I thought. My work was close to the Humane Society, so I would go over there on my lunch break and walk through, waiting for that one special dog to jump out at me, but I realized that my heart was just shut down from my past experience. It surprised me that I could walk through there so many times without so much as wanting to play with any of the dogs.

Then one Saturday, my cousin and her daughter came over and we all went to the shelter. They picked out a few, but then there was Leroy, who was such a sweet dog and so good with her daughter. I liked him right away. He was fuzzy and had a broken tail. He was funny looking, but I took him just the same. It took a long time for me to name him and I know now it was just another problem I had with commitment. My experience with the previous dog had broken my heart and I had also recently gone through a rough break up, another reason for starting a new life in Kentucky. I was pretty fragile. I see now that Leroy and I saved each other. He, with his broken tail and about to be put down, and me with my broken heart that needed to heal, were meant for each other. My cousin later told me that she wasn't going to let me leave that day without taking a dog home with me. I can't imagine my life without Leroy.

TJ was quite a different story. I was helping another cousin, who rescues dogs, because she had a house full, so I took him in to foster and he and Leroy hit it off. They are best buddies.

Personality Plus

Leroy somehow decided that his way of giving you a hug is to walk between your legs. I have to warn people, especially men, so he doesn't take them by surprise. He knows the words, "give me a hug" and obliges! He also watches TV. I have heard of some dogs that do that, but he really watches it. If a dog comes on the screen he starts barking. Now that TJ is in the house it is a little different game, because Leroy will see the dog on TV and TJ will hear it. Then everyone is barking and it is mayhem at our house! People always comment on how sweet, cool, and laid back Leroy is, and I consider myself extremely lucky.

I currently volunteer with the Shamrock Organization, and my mom and I recently volunteered with a Kentucky dog transport (also called an underground railroad) to take dogs to their new homes and shelters in other states. Having Leroy and TJ in my life, and the volunteer work I do, have been such positive experiences and have made me whole.

- Nicole Harmon

Leroy and TJ

Lucille Louise

I met Lucille Louise, or Lucy Lou for short, and fell in love with her and her puppies. She was so small, just a fraction over four pounds, when I first saw her at a shelter in Washington, DC.

When the rescue organization got her they found out she was pregnant again and terminated the pregnancy. When I went in, I wasn't sure at first if I would get one of the puppies or the momma. They were all precious toy rat terriers. It took a few visits, but one time when I went in, I was holding her and she finally stopped shaking then fell asleep in my arms. I knew that was my girl.

Since Lucy Lou and her two puppies were so small, the rescue league only took one application and tried to move the dogs quickly to find them good homes. She was so small that I nicknamed her Peanut, even though now she's a whopping six and a half pounds.

She shook in my arms for the first month and a half and

didn't play for about five months, but it seems that every month she is feeling more and more comfortable. A typical terrier, she loves to bark at other dogs walking by. She is not a big fan of kids, but is slowly starting to be more social with other dogs. She has a play date almost every day with her best friend, Maude, a miniature rat terrier, and her boyfriend, Bo, an 11-year-old yellow Labrador.

Lucy Lou is definitely a momma's girl and loves to go with me wherever I go. It is easy since she is small, as she just stays in her bag and doesn't make a peep. No one really knows she is with me unless she gets an itch and the bag shakes, or they see her looking out of the bag.

She loves her treats and is really good at begging. She also is a good soccer player. We play squeak ball with a little soccer ball all the time. She loves to play with her bones. We play fetch with her bones, and she buries them or chews them to pieces.

Lucy Lou is not my first dog, but she is the first dog I've ever adopted. It was a great experience and if I ever decide to get another dog, I would definitely get a rescue dog again.

- Linda Merrill

Maggie

We found Maggie, a six-week-old border collie mix, at an animal shelter in Georgia. We wanted a puppy as a playmate for our six-year-old son. We had two dogs prior to Maggie, but we had never adopted a dog.

We actually chose another dog before Maggie. There were two puppies at the shelter that were from the same litter. Maggie was very loud and yappy, as if to say, "look at me, look at me," while the other one sat quietly and looked at us so sweetly. We decided on the sweet one, and were ready to adopt her, but were then told that she was already spoken for, so we adopted the noisy one. When we took her home, we were driving a station wagon, and Maggie bounced around and played in the back the whole way home. She was full of energy, frisky and fun, from day one.

Maggie loves to fetch, and when she was younger she would chase a Frisbee until her tongue was lying on the ground. The only thing wrong with her fetching was that she loved to drop it just out of reach and then stand in her fetch mode waiting for you to retrieve it and throw it again. She would always wear us out before she would get tired.

Maggie is crazy about birthday parties. Whenever we bring out a cake, candles blazing and people singing "Happy Birthday," she joins in, barking the song.

I know everyone thinks their dog is smart, and Maggie is no different. Being mostly border collie and well-trained from the start, she really is a smart dog. She knows over 80 words. She can retrieve any toy from her toy basket when we ask for it by name. She can also retrieve the newspaper from the driveway, which is especially nice on rainy mornings.

She was very easy to train. She will stop at the end of the yard or driveway and sit and wait for you to get the object that you accidentally threw into the road. Even now that she is an old lady of 15, she still loves to go for morning walks and she loves to play tug-of-war at supper time. She is a wonderful, delightful addition to our family.

- Sarah Chalpan

Maggie is Titan's cousin and they have grown up together. They have had numerous sleepovers throughout the years. Maggie is Titan's oldest and dearest friend.

Matilda

When I went to PetSmart I had no intention of adopting that day, even though I had been thinking about adopting a dog for a while. However, one look at Matilda and she stole my heart. The shelter had several dogs there that day, and Matilda (then named Greta) stood up at the side of her crate and looked at me with big brown eyes. And she kept getting more convincing. I read on her crate that she was about four years old and housetrained. The more I learned about her, the more I knew I had to bring her home with me.

I have had dogs all of my life. Growing up we had purebreds. As an adult, I've always had mixed breeds who were rescues or who came to me in some other fashion. I had never been through a formal adoption and I found it to be very professional and thorough, as I gave them information about me and my home, and made an appointment to go back to pick her up. Matilda had not been with them long, as she had been at the pound and rescued by this organization. She was checked by a vet and then came home to live with me.

My aunt once had a dachshund named Matilda and I thought it was fitting for my new dachshund-mix companion. Her full name is Matilda Grace Scratchabelly of the Royal Scratchabellies. The rest of her name came from one of her favorite things, and she is a bit regal, and yes, spoiled.

She was so frightened when she first came home. She was afraid of people and dogs and liked quiet. When company would come over she would run and hide. She had previously been given away or dumped several times, we think, and she was very insecure. I could not tell her "no" in a sharp tone. She might have even been abused at some point.

Soon Matilda came out of her shell and within the first few months began to feel safer and became more social. She has her quirks, like all dogs. She is very particular about where she does her business. For the first several years I would actually have to drive her to the vet's yard for her to do her thing. Even now, she won't do her business in her own yard, she has to go for a walk. She's become very curious and her terrier nose gets the best of her sometimes.

She is very protective and worries about me. I've had some fainting spells in the past and when I nap on the couch it makes her a little nervous. At first I can feel her staring at me. Then she puts her front paws up on the sofa, and if I haven't moved by then, she'll bark. It is not because she wants to go out, eat or play. She just wants to make sure I will wake up.

Her sleep habits are interesting. She likes to go to bed at a certain time and has a bed in my bedroom. If I stay up past her bedtime reading or watching television, she will come out of the bedroom into the living room to tell me it's time to come to bed. She'll continue this periodically until I go to bed.

Matilda has made some very good doggie friends. Lula

Mae, a Jack Russell terrier mix, is her best friend and if the door is open at Lula Mae's house, Matilda will go right in to play. Lula Mae barks as other dogs pass, but if she sees Matilda, she whines because she wants to play. I have a new fence, so Lula Mae can come over for play dates in the back yard. Matilda's other good friend is a border collie. Matilda used to be more afraid of larger dogs, and so her friendship with Chi is quite special. Chi is a service dog and even visited me in the hospital once. We live in a great neighborhood for doggie friends.

I'm so glad that Matilda feels safe and secure, and has become a social, loving dog. She was that way with me from the beginning. Matilda stole my heart that first day and continues to be a blessing to me every day.

- Mary Ann Norman

Daffy

Moe

Moe was my first adopted dog, but certainly not my first rescue dog, as I had rescued dogs for years. I was newly married and my wife had a poodle, a rescue dog from Tennessee, who was old and on her last leg, so to speak. I was afraid my wife would be devastated if anything happened to Jodie. So, thinking I would fill the gap that Jodie's loss might create, I went down to a Gwinnett Humane Society adoption event. I found 10 puppies in a corral and there was one big dopey one named Moe. His parents weren't that big and we wanted about a 40-pound dog. Moe could be adopted at eight weeks old, and there he was, with brindle-colored, wavy hair. I took him home and Moe, a chow/pit bull mix, grew into a 100-pound dog. His neck was huge and his size was intimidating, but he would whine, cry and always had to snuggle up to his stuffed animals, carry them around and sleep with them.

Jodie, who was just eight pounds, was definitely the

alpha dog. They became buddies and Jodie stayed with us for another few years. She loved her big brother and also loved to be the dominant one.

Moe turned out to be the sweetest dog ever. Our son was born around the time we adopted Moe and he was very protective. Moe was always good with all of our future dogs and was basically just a big baby. When Jodie passed away, Moe became king of the household. We rescued another dog, Macie, from Tennessee, a 30-pound, long-haired mutt. She and Moe became buddies. We added a 12-foot x 12-foot room to our house for the two dogs so they could have more space.

Then came Daffy, a young, snappy little dog. Moe and Macie quickly showed him who was boss. Daffy was an abused puppy that I found in a box where I worked. He is a nervous dog and diabetic, and he needed us. We created a diet for him of special prescription food. When we created a pet soup kitchen so that other dogs don't need to starve, and so hopefully people don't have to give up their pets, we named it after Daffy.

- Tom Wargo

Daffy's Pet Soup Kitchen

Tom Wargo, founder and CEO of Daffy's Pet Soup Kitchen and The SOS Club, is Daffy's, Moe's, Macie's, and numerous other dogs' and cats' father. A builder by trade, he landed many contractor jobs for seniors and folks in need. Many people he worked for had companion animals and were struggling to feed them, so he began carrying pet food with him to the job sites and distributing food from his work truck. Some of these people were barely able to feed themselves, yet they would share what little they had with their pets. For some, these pets were their whole lives, and this resonated with Tom. So he began buying and giving out more and more pet food. His business calls turned into calls from people who needed help with their pets.

Prompted by their love and devotion to animals, he and his wife founded the SOS (Save our Souls) Club to assist the community, families and pets. Daffy's Pet Soup Kitchen was born a few years after that and is the largest pet food bank in Georgia, and the only one with multiple locations. They have a warehouse where they store and distribute food as needed to more than 2,000 pets every month, and the need continues to grow each day. By feeding pets, they are able to help them stay with their families. They also supply food to animal shelters so they can extend the amount of time animals can stay there, increasing their chances for adoption.

Daisy's Dog House

They also have a dog named Daisy, who was adopted as a puppy from an abusive situation where she was unwanted and kept outside. They started Daisy's Dog House because they heard about a woman in Georgia who refused to abandon her pets and felt trapped into living in an abusive home. The shelters would not offer her and her animals a place to stay and she knew that if she left them behind they would be abused. The mission of Daisy's Dog House is to build kennels at domestic violence centers so these women do not have to make the choice of leaving their pets behind or risking their lives.

Newman

Newman was not quite three years old when we saw him at a shelter in Charleston, SC. We had looked for a greyhound on the Internet first, searching for a red brindle, and found two of them at this particular shelter. Greyhounds can have any of 16 different colors and coats, so we were being very specific by wanting a red brindle. We had a greyhound before, and because of all the problems that greyhounds encounter and the lives they lead as racers we wanted to adopt another one.

Adopting Newman was a wonderful experience, as the people at the shelter were professional, thorough and loving. It was a tough decision choosing between Newman and the other red brindle greyhound. Newman seemed to be more outgoing and wagged his tail a million miles an hour. We later found out that wasn't a good trait, as he had a disease dogs develop called "happy tail". He later had stitches to correct it, and it was a mess for several months.

Newman's previous life was at a track in Melbourne, FL. He raced in trial races and retired early following just seven races. Between the track and greyhound organizations, Newman, like all greyhounds, spent some time in a foster home program. There he learned to live in a house, which included learning about mirrors and TVs (not to try to run through them) and learning not to "counter cruise." Greyhounds are such large, athletic dogs that it is very easy for them to help themselves to things on countertops.

At first Newman was wary, and we suspected he had been abused. It turns out he was, and he continues to be more skittish around me than my wife. He did adjust rather quickly, faster than Harley, our first greyhound, and got into the flow of things in no time.

Typical Greyhound

All greyhounds like to run, so we need to keep him leashed. He occasionally pays visits to the neighbors, but fortunately he doesn't run too far. He is actually a real couch potato and sleeps a good 18 hours a day. Greyhounds are known not to bark, and this holds true for Newman. He is a mellow, gentle dog and very good with children. He is aloof when it comes to other dogs. Being a short-haired dog, he is very low maintenance, needing a bath just twice a year. People think that greyhounds are high maintenance because they are runners, but Newman is quite happy with a long walk in the morning and a modest walk in the afternoon. He has energy spurts where he will be very active for about five minutes, playing with his squeaky toys, and then just as quickly goes and lies down for a nap.

Newman was trained as a therapy dog. He is quiet, easy to control, and just the right height for a wheelchair or the side of a bed. Newman is still young, as he still has some puppy in him, so we will wait a few more years to begin doing visits.

    We will always adopt dogs. Before we fell in love with greyhounds, we had old English sheepdogs.

- Bill Putnam

Pandy

A Jack Russell/bichon frisé mix, with possible West Highland terrier in her, Pandy was adopted when she was about a year old. It had been a while since we had adopted a dog. We previously had two other dogs from the Humane Society of Johnson County in Franklin, IN. When we were ready for another dog, we went back again and found Pandy.

I have strong feelings against puppy mills, and I feel like giving a home to a pet that needs one makes more sense than getting one for status. I have also always felt that mixed breeds have better personalities, and they seem to be healthier dogs.

Pandy was easy to adopt. We had a background with the organization and had a good rapport with the people there. I was also impressed with the fact that they called back to check on how things were going after the adoption process and offered support if needed. We had to sign a contract that if we decided to get rid of the dog we would contact them first so they could take her back.

The Kids Before Pandy

Our first dog, Lacey, was totally unexpected. We weren't looking to get a dog. Our two oldest girls were four and two at the time. My neighbor was fostering Lacey, and she looked so much like my childhood dog, Boilermaker, that I couldn't resist. She was a fabulous family pet for 13 years. After Lacey came Molly, who was one of 10 puppies that were left at the Humane Society on Christmas. Every Thursday they have an event where you can go visit with the pets that are up for adoption. We filled out the paperwork earlier in the week and got approved and brought Molly home. The girls didn't remember how difficult a puppy was, because they were so young during Lacey's puppy months. We plugged through Molly's first two years and lost a few shoes, had to redo and replace some furniture, etc. Unfortunately, Molly was part of a tragedy and we found ourselves without a pet. One of my daughters convinced me to let her get rabbits, which turned out to be a short-lived and awful idea. We found a good home for the rabbits and started our search for another dog.

We found Pandy on the Humane Society of Johnson County's website and called to see if they would bring her to the event the following Thursday. When we got there, an older woman was filling out an application for Pandy. She had fallen in love with her. She told me that her husband had died and she was now ready to get a pet, and Pandy was just perfect for her. I was fine with that, but my daughter was not. The woman finally said that it was only fair that we take her since we had already filled out the application and made claim to her. Later, after we were home with Pandy, the Humane Society called to tell us that the woman wanted us to know that she had picked out another dog and was sure this one was better for her and didn't want us to worry about her. We were grateful all the way around.

Pandy was an adjustment for us. We had only had experience with big dogs, so having a small–and yes, a bit needy–dog was new to us. She likes to snuggle and to be right on or next to people. She sleeps on pillows or on the top of furniture, like a cat. She doesn't quite understand the concept of fetch. We throw the ball and she runs to it, picks it up, brings it back, and then it becomes a game of keep away. She has to be in whatever room somebody else is in, and if you are the only one home she just follows you around like a shadow. And Pandy is quite social. In fact, she has a Facebook page where you can see lots of pictures created by the girls. Her one flaw is licking. We are working on it, but it's evidently her thing. There are a lot worse flaws she could have, so we feel blessed!

- Sherry Vanderbush Bujarsky

Penny

Penny is the first dog that I've owned myself, and I adopted her when she was about seven months old. I have always loved dogs, and I yearned for the day I would call one my own. I loved my family's basset hound, but owning a dog as an adult is quite a different thing. After college graduation, I knew it was time for me to find my dog. I've always supported shelters and rescue organizations, so that's where I started. I wasn't interested in pedigree or breed standards. I just wanted a good companion.

The adoption experience with Penny was a great one, and it happened so quickly. I started looking for dogs on Petfinder.com. I made a trip to an adoption day to see a specific dog, but she had already been adopted. Shortly after, I saw a photo of a beagle, which was one of the breeds I liked, at a nearby shelter. She was in someone's arms at the time, and she looked petrified. But I also thought she looked sweet and cute. I called the shelter and asked if the dog was still there. They told me she was, and that a woman from a local rescue group had inquired about the dog, too, and was planning to come get her that day. I hung up the phone, got in my car with my then-boyfriend, Adam, (now husband) and drove to the shelter.

When Adam and I went to the shelter, I didn't specifically ask to see Penny, though she was the dog I had seen online. I thought I would look around first, and keep an eye out for her. This particular shelter didn't name the dogs; instead they were numbered. But I had already named her. The shelter employees first showed us puppies. They took us to a puppy-specific room, then to an area with a litter of shepherd-mix puppies. Finally they took us to see all the other dogs. We walked down a long path with pens on both sides of us. The dogs were going crazy, barking and jumping up on their pen doors. It was loud.

About halfway down the hall, I looked over and saw the little beagle from Petfinder. She was wiggling around, looking half-excited to see people and half-terrified of all the barking noise. I asked to see her, and the shelter employee took her out for us. She was so happy to get out of her pen. They took us to a fenced yard where we could run around and spend time with her. Within 15 minutes I was ready to sign the adoption papers! I liked Penny's personality. She was happy to run around and play with Adam, but she was also calm and happy to just sit with us. She is still exactly that way five years later.

Penny's Eating "Disorder"

Like most beagles, Penny will do anything for food. Really, she's shameless. One time I was petting her in bed with the lights off, and I smelled something strange. "Something smells like Desitin," I said to my husband. I turned on the light, and Penny's face was white. She had gotten a bottle of rash cream off my nightstand and had a good time with it. Panicked, my husband called the Poison Control number on the back of the Desitin bottle. The woman from Poison Control was unalarmed and explained they get several calls each day about babies and dogs eating it. She said it was nothing to be worried about and that she'll probably get sick, but she'll be fine. She did, indeed, throw up a short time later.

One time, Penny threw up in her crate, and it turned out she had eaten a confetti bat from Halloween. Another time, I had a few friends over around Christmas, and we went out to a movie after dinner. When we came home at about midnight there were Ghirardelli chocolate wrappers all over the floor. I had left a small dish of chocolate squares on the coffee table. Penny had eaten about seven of them. Funny thing is, there were also candy bells in the dish, but Penny only ate the high-quality stuff. We called our vet, and he said the kind and the amount of chocolate eaten wasn't toxic. She didn't even get sick. She probably thought it was the best day ever. Recently Penny got into a bag of hot dog buns at my mom's house and ate the entire package.

Other than food, Penny's other "Penny-ism" is that her favorite spot in the house is under our bed. She lies under it with her back legs and tail sticking out. I imagine she feels safe, but wants to keep part of herself out in case she needs to get out quickly and see what there is to eat!

Penny is a true delight and I'm so glad that the first dog I own is an adopted dog. I will definitely adopt again. There are so many amazing animals in need of homes.

- Hannah Carroll

Pepper

We wanted a playmate for our one-year-old mutt Trinka, who we had gotten as a puppy from a friend. At the time we were living in Miami, FL, and we went to a no-kill shelter there to look at all the dogs. Pepper, a one-year-old black mixed chow/Labrador retriever, was about the size of Trinka and he seemed very friendly. We decided quickly to adopt him, and it was a good adoption experience.

Pepper seemed excited at the shelter, and we thought he was just that — excited. But when we brought him home, we learned about his fear-based aggression. At first he would snap and bark at Trinka, who put him in his place. Trinka quickly showed him who was the alpha dog, and Pepper enjoyed his place in our family from that time forward.

In Pepper's first week at our house he dug out from under the fence. He wandered off about a half of a mile where a woman found him and took him back to the shelter, and they scanned his microchip. We got the call from the shelter and off we went to bring Pepper back home. He tried over and over to dig out, curious about what was on the other side of the fence, but we were wise to him by then and it was a long time and a different fence before he dug out again.

When Pepper was eight years old, he was hit by a car. We had moved from Miami to Atlanta, GA. Fortunately, the driver of the car saw him and slowed considerably; nonetheless, the collision was unavoidable. The impact sent him skidding on his back across the road and into a light post, flipping him back onto his feet. Without missing a beat, he lunged at the car, barking and snarling, snapping at the tires and front bumper. As the adrenaline burned off, he limped into the yard and collapsed at my feet, trembling. He spent the night at the emergency vet and was home the next day, very sore, but none the worse, considering.

We loved the goofy looks he would give us, one ear up, the other flopped over. If we tried to get a picture of him though, his expression would change. In almost all of our photographs of him, he looks as if he's just been beaten. He was always very skittish; scaring easily with a light touch to his rump. He hated having his feet touched, but would melt with a chest rub.

Best described as endearingly stupid, we loved Pepper so much. A co-worker of Lisa's, named Tanya, lived in the neighborhood and had become the dogs' caretaker when we were out of town. One Sunday morning, a few months after moving to Savannah, he dug out from under the backyard fence. With Trinka following, they set out into the neighborhood. Soon there was a knock on our front door. Standing at the door were Trinka and Tanya. Tanya explained she happened to look out of her window and saw two very familiar looking dogs sniffing around her front yard. She went out and they immediately recognized her. She opened her car door, and they bounded in for the ride home. Once here, however, Pepper refused to leave her car.

One time Bill locked himself out of our house. He knocked on the door, thinking maybe Lisa was home. Pepper came to the door, looked at Bill, yawned and turned around. I guess he knew he couldn't unlock the door, so he just went back to his nap.

Some of Pepper's fears stayed with him all of his life. He had a strong fear of thunderstorms. When it stormed, which happens a lot on the coast, he would hide under our desks at our feet while we were working. When he saw another dog, even little ones, he would bark, but hide behind his sister, Trinka. He became more scared after Trinka passed away. She was his protector.

Pepper developed what seemed like narcolepsy. In his later years he would be standing there, looking at us, and all of a sudden fall over, seemingly sound asleep. Minutes later, he would get up and go about his business. We're not sure if it really was narcolepsy or if he just got tired.

Above all, Pepper was a sweet dog, who came into our lives and gave us unconditional love and many happy memories. Pepper lived to be 19 years old. For a 60-pound dog, our friends and veterinarian found this quite remarkable. Trinka lived to be 17, and our two cats, which also grew up with our dogs, lived into their 20s. People joke about wanting to be our pets when they come back in another life. We're not sure how we are so lucky to have such a long time with all of our pets, but we do feel blessed!

- Bill and Lisa Ballard

Lucie and Roadie

Roadie and Lucie

Roadie came into our lives four years before his sister, Lucie. Roadie, a Labrador retriever/white shepherd mix, was a little over a year old when we adopted him, and Lucie, a Jack Russell terrier/Labrador retriever mix was just four months old. I love dogs, and these two were meant to be a part of our family. Roadie was the first dog I have ever adopted, and both his and Lucie's adoption experiences were fantastic.

First Came Roadie

We found Roadie through a network of caring people who fostered rescue dogs in Bluffton, SC. A friend of mine was involved in this network and told me about a dog being fostered at Marthie Sumner's home. Marthie works at the Coastal Veterinary Clinic and has a real heart for dogs and all animals. We wanted an older dog, and when we arrived at Marthie's house all the dogs came over to us immediately, except one. Marthie said she would have to coax Roadie, as he was very shy. A few minutes later a very large, very beautiful white dog came over to us, sniffed us, gave us a kiss, and sat down between us. We knew when he walked in the room he was ours. The kiss sealed the deal.

To this day he is still a little shy. Roadie is petrified of thunder and has separation anxiety. He has become king of the beach, as inevitably someone always stops to ask about him, pet him and tell us he is beautiful. Countless people have called him regal. He also loves to pose for pictures on the beach—until he has had enough, of course, and then he won't even look at you. When he's not posing for pictures, he is guarding his dad, who is a professional photographer. Roadie is a very protective dog. We have never had to leash him, as he would never leave our side.

There is one exception, and that's when his girlfriend, Sunny, is around. A part-time Hilton Head Island resident, Sunny lives near us on the beach. She is a Labrador retriever, and she and Roadie became fast friends from the moment they met. I have never seen Roadie take to a dog like he did with Sunny, and they can spend the entire day running and playing. In fact, it was Sunny who got Roadie to go into the ocean for the first time. He would be content to sit and watch the other dogs play and swim, but by the second day Sunny went for a swim, he joined her.

Next Came Lucie

One day I stopped by Maranatha Farm in Ridgeland, SC, on my way home from the airport to say hello to its founder, Karen Wilkins, and there was an adorable little white puppy. When I took her out of the crate, Karen said she had just been adopted. After playing with her for a bit, I sadly put her back in the crate, and told Karen if anything happened with the adoption to let me know. Luckily for me, she called a week later and said the person couldn't take her because the place she lived was requiring an exorbitant non-refundable pet deposit.

The next day I was on my way to Maranatha to get my perfect puppy! Of course, this all hinged on whether Roadie accepted this adorable baby. Roadie gave her the big sniff down and she seemed to pass. To make up for bringing a sister into the house, we gave Roadie more attention than usual for many weeks, and now they don't like to be without each other. Other than Sunny, Lucie is Roadie's best friend, and he's a terrific big brother.

There are so many dogs in need of a forever home. Since I can't bring them all home, and my two bring me pure joy, I do what I can by volunteering for Maranatha Farm. Karen and her husband, Dwayne, have a wonderful farm, and I enjoy helping them out with fundraising and social networking. Karen and Dwayne's dedication to rescuing and finding homes for the dogs is inspiring. In Dwayne's spare time, with the help of a few volunteers, he makes custom-fitted wheelchairs for handicapped animals and provides them at no cost. Pet owners are only asked to pay for shipping, if they can afford it, and to send him a photo of the dog using the wheelchair.

- Laura Hobbs

Lucie and Roadie

Rory

Rory was three years old when we adopted him from the Tennessee Valley Golden Retriever Rescue in Knoxville, TN. Rory is a golden retriever, and his name fits him perfectly, as Rory means "red king," and he is very red for a golden retriever. He is a large retriever, weighing in at 96 pounds, and he's not fat. He's just plain big all over: taller, bigger head, bigger feet, thicker ears, and longer tail. It's nice having a dog I can pet without bending over at all.

When we adopted Rory we had just lost another golden retriever, Clancy, to autoimmune hemolytic anemia, a disease that destroys the red blood cells. We also adopted Clancy from the Tennessee Valley Golden Retriever Rescue.

Prior to Clancy, we had another dog from a private rescue from an abusive home—a golden retriever puppy, six months old, about whom my daughter had heard from a co-worker. She immediately volunteered to take the puppy. The co-worker asked, "Don't you think you should check with your mother first?" and my daughter replied, "Oh, you don't know my mom!" I wasn't planning on acquiring another dog at that point, but I agreed to take the puppy until we could find him a good home. Eleven years later, when he passed away, we were still looking.

Adopting Rory was practically automatic since we had a previous dog from the shelter. We didn't have to do the home visit or interview since they already knew us. I also volunteer with this organization, although not as much as I'd like. I'd adopt another dog or take in a foster dog, but my husband has put his foot down. He knows the house would be full of dogs if I had my way!

We first heard about Rory through the rescue group. I called a few days after we lost Clancy, and they had just found out about a male golden discovered wandering along Interstate 40 in semi-rural Tennessee. Jess, a vet student at the University of Tennessee, found him. Rory was emaciated and had a terrible flea problem. In fact, when Jess took him to her own vet, he said he had never seen such a bad case of fleas. When I heard his story, I knew we could help him feel loved and wanted again.

It was more than a month before we could get all the paperwork done and arrange a pick-up with Jess and our adoption coordinator, Kathy. We arrived at the designated place way ahead of time. When Jess and Rory got there, Rory was glad to meet us, but reluctant to leave Jess. For several days after we got him home, he kept going to my car as if to say, "Well, it's been great, guys, but I really want to go home to Jess now."

As far as we have been able to piece together, Rory spent most of his previous life in either a kennel or a crate. As a result, he is now terrified of crates. When we got him, he had huge calluses on his elbows and had broken most of his front teeth off by chewing on something. The vets suspect it was a crate door or gate. When we took him to be neutered a few days after he moved in with us, the vet also had to extract seven of his incisors. The nerves were exposed, and he was in pain from them. It was hard for him to eat.

Rory loves to ride in cars. In fact he loves it more than any of the seven dogs I've had in the past. Part of that is due to separation anxiety, I think. It's still very difficult to get out of the house without him. I have to bribe him with a Kong full of something yummy or a handful of little treats scattered around the kitchen floor. The hardest and saddest thing, though, is that when we go on our periodic trips to Chicago to visit family and friends, he is terrified of leaving the car. We can coax him out at a rest stop, but as soon as he's done his business, he drags me back to the car and whines to get inside. That's what makes us think he was dumped along the interstate. He doesn't act like that if we go anywhere else—only when we're close to a highway.

One of our games is racing upstairs. I head up the front stairs, and Rory takes the back stairway. Surprisingly, despite my bad hips, I usually win. My edge is that he has to decide which of his many puppy toys to bring with him. That gives me a head start.

Rory also has a game he plays with one of our cats. The rules are that she comes into the bathroom with me when I'm getting ready for bed, and he positions himself between the bed and the bathroom door. Once I'm in bed, she "sneaks" out of the bathroom, slowly sliding along the wall, eyes locked with Rory's the whole time. At some point, maybe 10 to 20 minutes later, she makes a huge leap onto the bed while he tries to catch her. Once she's on the bed, the game is over, and we can all settle down. Needless to say, I've been startled a few times while reading when a cat comes flying through the air and a huge dog jumps up after her!

Rory has been just about the perfect dog, with only a few "accidents" in the house. He doesn't get into the trash, he only chews on his own toys (and thanks to his lack of front teeth, he can't disembowel his stuffed toys), and he even "asks permission" to get up on the bed. Unfortunately, lately he has discovered the rewards of taking food off the kitchen counter after my husband left out a couple of hamburgers. Oh, well, nobody–not even Rory or my husband–is perfect.

There's an extra something special about rescue dogs that is very endearing. They understand what you've done for them, and they are very grateful. Will I adopt another rescue dog some day? Absolutely! That's the only way I'd ever get a dog.

- Marjie O'Connor

Shadow

Our Labrador retriever, Shadow, was six weeks old when we adopted him. We didn't have any other dogs at the time and had promised the kids that when we settled in from our last military transfer we would buy a home and get a dog.

I had heard that PetSmart hosted adoption weekends from a local animal shelter. Project Hope from Metropolis, IL, brought the dogs over the bridge of the Ohio River to Paducah, KY. We had several criteria for the dog we would adopt, and I was sure it would take months to find a yellow male Labrador. I had wanted a yellow Lab because when we were stationed at USCG Training Center in Two Rock, CA, there were a few families that raised and trained Labradors from six weeks old through 18 months old for the Seeing Eye Dog Program. I knew if there was any dog I would like to be around, a Labrador would be it. At the time I was not a dog person, so of course it took them only two short weeks to find our Shadow! Our son, who was five years old at the time, named him Shadow because he watched the movie *Homeward Bound* over and over again.

Shadow really got into my heart and I have to admit, I was quite fond of him from the start. I worry about him like he is one of our children. I never thought I would be that way with a dog. The last two Jeeps I have purchased had to be big enough in the back for him to travel with us. Like any good dog parent, my life is greatly influenced by Shadow.

After adopting Shadow I found out that I am allergic to dogs. Dealing with allergies was nothing new for me, but having a dog brought on new challenges for me. I know all of the things allergists tell you to do, but that just wasn't going to work for me. Shadow has his bed in the master bedroom, so we got rid of the carpeting. He has to stay clean and is an inside dog, which really helps. He still goes outside to play with his buddy, Premo, a neighbor's pit bull. Shadow loves going for walks and seems to be taking us for walks instead of the other way around. Everything that Shadow brings to our family life certainly outweighs any allergy problems.

Shadow's basic training skills were taught to him mostly by our daughter. Since no one in the family knew what to do, we bought a book and read up on raising a puppy. It helped us greatly!

Shadow the Entertainer

Shadow is a natural entertainer. He will only "sing" to the songs "Jesus Loves Me" played from a stuffed toy puppy and "Who Let the Dogs Out," another lesson learned from our daughter. They both have varied taste in music. For some reason he has an issue with Sponge Bob Square Pants' show, or at least he is very sensitive to the music, which he can hear from two floors away. When he hears the music for the show he runs down to the TV and barks as if to make it stop. He does the usual shaking paw trick, except he is a bit more advanced. When you say "shake your paw" he shakes with his right one and then you say "other paw" and he gives you the left one. He will do this several times, but only if you have a good treat. He will also balance treats on his nose then catch them.

Shadow the Scholar

He is a very bright dog. There are so many commands and words he knows that it is hard to recall them all. He can spell over 10 words, and some of his favorites are w-a-l-k, c-o-o-k-i-e, and j-e-e-p. There are also many phrases that he knows. Shadow can count to six and knows over 50 words. Some words that really get his attention are French fries, leash, daddy, ride, bone, and of course, cookie. He knows what I am thinking sometimes, as he responds by going to the cookie jar, the door or looking out the window for someone to come in.

When Shadow isn't entertaining us or showing off how smart he is, he is my very dear companion. When I had to retire due to health issues, this wonderful, loving dog was there for me. He has been by my side, helping me to adjust to this new challenge in my life. It was devastating to stop working, and Shadow helped cheer me up with his goofy smile. When the rest of the family is at work and school he is there so I don't feel lonely, and when weather permits he goes with me to town to run errands.

- Millie Walter Baier

Toby and Shasta

Shasta, Toby and Cooper

We adopted brother and sister, Toby and Shasta, when they were four and a half months old, and were as cute as could be—part St. Bernard, part Collie and who knows what else! We adopted them from an organization in the Midwest, but they were actually born hundreds of miles away.

They were first taken to a shelter in Nebraska, but the shelter did not have room for them and could not take them in. A help notice was sent out to all Midwestern St. Bernard Rescue groups, as the dogs were part St. Bernard. One group said they could take the pups and place them with a foster family until they were adopted. The pups were driven across country by many dedicated volunteers.

We saw their pictures on Petfinder.com and thought they were really cute. My husband saw them first, and I think he knew right away, but I didn't. We were looking for only one dog and initially adopted Shasta. Three days later we went back for Toby!

The adoption process with Shasta and Toby was extensive, including a lengthy application, references checked, a call to our vet, as well as a home inspection and lots of waiting. They were definitely worth the effort–we love them so much!

We have always adopted from rescue or shelter groups because there are too many wonderful dogs out there without homes. It is so sad to think of all the unwanted dogs living in cages. It breaks my heart when I think about it. Our previous dogs, Dakota and Hunter, were adopted too, when they were puppies.

Mr. Cooper

The latest member of our family is Cooper, a Newfoundland mix, who was just 12 weeks old when we adopted him. Like Shasta and Toby, we first saw him on Petfinder.com. My husband saw his picture, along with his siblings, under the description of Newfoundland pups. We love big dogs and he looked so sweet. He was hard to forget. We decided a few days later to make the six-hour drive down to southern Illinois to see him. By the time we arrived, he was the only one left of his litter of five. All of the rest had been adopted by families in North Carolina, Ohio and Indiana.

The minute the folks at the shelter put Cooper in my arms, I knew we would adopt him. We noticed how calm he was, especially for a puppy. The woman at the rescue group said his whole litter was quiet and settled. I held him for a few minutes and then gave him to my daughter to hold. He was a sweetheart from the beginning. His adoption process was just the opposite of Shasta and Toby's. It was very quick with very little paperwork.

The woman who rescued him gave him a bath and we took him home. He rode home nestled between my two daughters in the back seat and slept most of the way. The best part of that day was when we got home and the dogs started playing in the yard together. Cooper has been in love with Shasta ever since. Shasta has turned into quite a little mother to Cooper.

Cooper is a handsome dog. We love the patches of white on his chest and on a few of his toes. My daughter said it looked like he put his nose into powdered sugar because he has a little white on the tip of his nose. Cooper grew to be smaller than a purebred Newfoundland. He weighs in at 60 pounds at 10 months old. We think he was the runt of the litter. His full name is Cooper Bear, with nicknames Baby Bear and Cubbie. He is still calm, quiet and a little shy, like he was the first day we met him, which is just the opposite of his siblings, Shasta and Toby. Shasta and Toby are very loud, with lots of barking and big personalities.

Cooper is afraid of anything new or different. He is very cautious. Our favorite Cooper story is when we had him on our boat this summer and he was in the bow trying to see over the railing into the water. I kept holding onto his tail and hips. We had stopped the boat and were drifting. I couldn't believe Cooper was still pulling to look over the front of the boat because he's normally scared of everything. This went on for a few minutes, with Cooper straining to look over the front of the boat and me trying to stop him. Finally, my husband said to let go and see what happens. Cooper went head first over the bow of the boat into the water! He came up sputtering and my husband scooped him into the boat. My daughters were laughing so hard when Cooper fell in, and he looked pitiful as he was drying off. We were worried that he might not want to learn to swim, but after a few more days, he started wading into the water and started swimming. We still don't know what Cooper was trying to do, but it was so unlike his cautious personality that it makes us laugh every time we think about it.

Cooper is afraid of our Halloween decorations. We had to remove the big light-up pumpkins from our front porch this Halloween because Cooper was afraid to go in and out of the front door.

A handsome dog, he has a physical attribute that makes us laugh. Cooper has a really long tongue. I have never seen such a long tongue on a dog. I've been told it's a Newfoundland trait, but we really don't know how he fits it into his mouth. His tongue, hanging sideways out of his mouth, always makes my daughters giggle. We love our dogs so much and they bring such joy into our lives.

- Danielle Neveaux Semler

Cooper

Sugar and her Siblings

Our first adopted dog came into our lives 15 years ago. Her name was Sugar, and we have been adopting dogs ever since.

Sugar (or "Suga" as my grandson, Seaver, still calls her—he had trouble with pronouncing the letter R), was a seven-year-old cocker spaniel. We had two dogs already—Madison, a one-year-old stray, and Shelsh, a two-year-old rescue. I went to the shelter that day to look for a smaller dog that would not be so overwhelming for my then two-year-old grandson. Our other two dogs were very large and very affectionate.

I did not want a cocker spaniel, because I had one for 14 years who didn't really like children and I heard that is typical of the breed. Since then, that hasn't been my experience. Sugar and Seaver were best friends from the start. Seaver took one look at Sugar and wanted to pet her. The people at the shelter in Asheville, NC, showed us to a small room so we could play with Sugar. Seaver sat on the floor and Sugar ran around the room several times, happy not to be caged. Then she ran up to Seaver, flopped on his lap, looked up at him, gave him several kisses, and then sat quietly. After a few minutes Seaver looked up at me and said this was our dog. We looked no further.

We think Sugar had been used for breeding. When we took her home she had no idea how to climb stairs. She didn't know her name or respond to our voices. We thought at first she might be deaf. That wasn't the case—nobody had ever taken the time to talk to Sugar.

Sugar lived with us for 12 years until the ripe old age of 19. She was the sweetest dog I have ever known, and I trusted her completely with all children.

Buddy

Four years after Sugar came into our lives we rescued Buddy. He was a six-week-old chow/golden retriever/akita mix. My daughter saw Buddy as she was leaving the house one day. She called to tell me that there were two puppies at the end of our driveway. At that time we had three dogs. Seaver and I went out to find them, and Buddy came right to us, but the other puppy was so scared we never got close. It was the middle of January, and the night we found them the temperature got below zero, and they probably would not have survived. I could tell that Buddy had chow in him, and that was a breed I was not comfortable with. However, like the cocker spaniel, we have learned that you can't judge a dog by its breed, and Buddy stole our hearts. He is one of the most intelligent dogs I have ever known. He is very protective and extremely loyal. He is my son's constant companion.

Next was Foster

One year after Buddy showed up in our driveway we found Foster on the side of the road. He was just four weeks old and a beautiful Australian shepherd-mix puppy. By then, the family had grown to five dogs. I was on my way to my first day of work in a new job and saw a very small dog lying on the side of the road. As I passed her, I knew I had to make sure that if she was alive, she got the help she needed to survive. As I walked toward her she opened her eyes. I got back to my car, sat her on my lap and took her to the vet. By the time I got to work my cream colored pants and shirt had been ruined by carrying the puppy and holding her on my lap. I was asked to go home.

Foster had two broken legs, a broken pelvic bone, and was covered in ticks. The vet didn't cast her bones for two weeks because they did not think she would live. They had to hand feed her for two weeks before she started eating on her own. The vet kept her on an IV for nearly a month.

She came to live with us when she was strong enough to leave the vet's. She recovered completely, and to see her run and play with our other dogs you would never know she ever had an injury.

Wild Dunes

When we found Wild Dunes at the Brother Wolf Animal Rescue in Asheville we had six dogs at that time, including Foster and Buddy. My reasoning for going to the shelter was that we had room for another dog. We have three dogs from this particular animal rescue, and I went there looking for a smaller inside dog. Wild Dunes caught my eye, and I'm not sure why. A 75-pound, large mixed-breed dog at a little over a year old, I learned that she had been in the shelter since she was born. Most of her litter died of Parvo. She had been adopted out five times and returned. To put it mildly, she had some problems.

Being an experienced dog owner, I thought I might be able to handle what others before me had not. She had, and still has, some challenging behaviors. But the most obvious quality about her is that she loves me beyond her ability to control herself! She just can't get enough love and attention. The first couple of months were extremely challenging, but I was determined to not give up on her like everyone else. And each day I'm so glad I didn't give up!

We've had up to 10 dogs in our home at any one time, and I don't regret a minute of my time with them. I look forward to all the dogs who will find their way into our hearts in the future.

- Debi Fleming

Wild Dunes

Sydney

Sydney, a purebred beagle, came to live with me by way of the J & K Canine Academy in High Springs, FL. She had been rescued from a shelter in central Florida and trained to detect the odor of live bed bugs. I had met another adorable beagle, Ellie, who had been trained to detect bed bugs. I was amazed at how Ellie could sniff out insects that were hidden in a vial under a mattress in record time. I kept thinking about this after I saw Ellie and thought this might be a great business for me.

Not only was I a dog lover at heart, but I was aware of the bed bug crisis threatening the travel industry. A few months later, I traveled to Florida to become certified by the National Entomology Scent Detection Canine Association (NESDCA.)

And along came Sydney. I can't imagine why anyone would have given her up. Sydney was chosen for me by the training staff. The first day of my training, I was led to her kennel run. She was frisky, hyper and so cute! I couldn't control her in the least. This was the first time I've ever had a rescue dog, and I would do it over and over again! In fact, since I found Sydney, I have rescued eight dogs from shelters in metropolitan Atlanta for J & K Canine Academy's training program.

In the fall of 2008, Sydney and I opened the doors of Quest K9 Detectives, the first NESDCA-certified canine bed bug detection agency in metro Atlanta. Sydney and I continue to provide our services to hotels, schools, businesses, and residences. I couldn't have asked for a better partner!

Sydney has surprised me many times with her ability to locate even one bed bug. On a recent hotel inspection, we were accompanied by a pest control inspector whose job it was to find evidence of the bed bugs once Sydney alerted to the scent of them. Sydney alerted on a queen bed in one of the rooms and to the frustration of the inspector, he could see no traces of bed bugs. After obtaining permission from the hotel manager to literally rip apart the box spring, he located one live bed bug nymph in the center of the box spring. I always had faith in my dog's ability, but that day my faith in her soared to new heights.

Sydney, however, is not all work and no play. She loves to play fetch and has a special fetish for socks. Our family learned the hard way not to ever leave socks lying on the floor.

One evening, while in a rather frisky mood, Sydney scooped up a sock in her mouth, ran behind a sofa with it and came out the other side with no sock at all. I looked behind the sofa and anywhere else I could think, and found no sock. A slow feeling of horror began to creep over me. She must have swallowed the sock in seconds flat. What to do at 10 p.m.? I called her trainer, who called his vet, and we decided to orally administer some vegetable oil, watch her carefully, and wait until morning. If necessary, we were ready to take her in for surgery. Needless to say, Sydney slept on our bed so we could observe her. Throughout the night, we slept very little and prayed a lot.

Early the next morning, my husband awoke to a soft, abrupt coughing sound. Alarmed, he turned on the lights and we could hardly believe our eyes. There, laid out right in front of Sydney, smooth and flat, was the (regurgitated) sock! It was much the worse for wear, but Sydney was unscathed and unconcerned. Our prayers had been answered. No socks will ever touch our floors again, unless they're attached to a foot!

- Adrienne Grabowski

Thurston

Thurston, a purebred Chihuahua and quite the alpha male, was our first experience with adoption. He was not our first dog, though, and we couldn't have been happier with the adoption process. Growing up, my family seemed to always find strays that would come to live with us. Thurston came from the Small Dog Rescue in Atlanta, GA. So many dogs need forever homes, and so finding ourselves with no dogs at the moment and just one cat, we set out to make a home for a dog.

We had two dogs previously--a Labrador retriever and a mutt, both relatively large dogs. A Chihuahua was the last dog I thought I would get. I thought they were snippy, but Thurston is a sweet, fun little dog and to know him is to love him.

We went to look at another dog that we had found, but they told us she may or may not get along with our cat. We went to another PetSmart adoption event to look at another dog, but the caregiver was a no-show. We then drove back to the original adoption site, where Small Dog Rescue was at a PETCO in Sandy Springs, GA, and they told us of a very special dog they had named Thurston. The woman, who was his caregiver, showed him to us, and we were hooked. We took him for a walk around the store, then outside, and went back in and told them we would take him.

Even at just two years old, he was the proud papa of five puppies, all of which, plus their momma, were given to the Small Dog Rescue from a shelter. This little family was given up by a woman who had a house full of Chihuahuas, but they seemed well cared for. We are happy to report that they were all adopted.

Thurston is a good traveler. He lies on his blanket in the back seat and doesn't move or make a sound. In fact he's like that wherever he is. Any time I pick him up and put him down somewhere, he stays.

He's an energetic dog, though, and loves to play, especially on the bed. He loves wearing his harness and gets excited just by seeing it. He jumps up to have it put on him. He loves walks and loves to play with our cat, Freeway, who is the same weight as Thurston. A small dog, the vet always comments on how muscular he is, with strong legs and a thick neck.

Thurston loves apples. He chews on green apples and hides them from us so he can chew on them and play with them later. He loves to walk around with one in his mouth. On our last trip to his veterinarian, our vet commented on Thurston's clean, white teeth, and asked us if we brushed them often. We told him about the apples and he laughed and thought that was a great way to keep his teeth in good condition.

- Steve Willis

Toby

Toby was two years old when he came to live with us from the Houston Sheltie Sanctuary. At the time we had two shelties, Lilly and Laddie Boy, also adopted from the sanctuary. We originally fostered two other dogs and interviewed prospective sheltie adoptees for the sanctuary. There are too many unwanted dogs due to puppy mills, and we try to help as many as our home can hold.

Toby's story is somewhat of a miracle, as Toby is a Katrina dog. Either the rescue league or the police found Toby, emaciated and unable to walk, and rushed him from New Orleans to a veterinary hospital in Houston, where he stayed until he was able to leave. Most of the Katrina dogs were found within two weeks, but it took a month to find Toby.

Having moved from New Orleans to Houston, and also having a heart for all dogs, and especially shelties, when the Houston Sheltie Sanctuary called me to see if we would serve as a foster home for Toby we said yes. When we picked him up they handed me the leash, but Toby still could not walk well. He was a skinny 12 pounds, tall and with very little muscle mass. He needed lots of love and someone to spoon feed him and help him go to the bathroom. The poor little thing could not even lift his leg without falling over, so he would lean against us for support.

At first we fed him anything he would eat, including a roast, lean steak and steamed vegetables. Slowly, and with the help of Lilly and Laddie Boy, Toby was walking on his own after two weeks, keeping up with the pack and making friends with our cats. Lilly and Laddie Boy took care of Toby and were really sweet to him, and the cats got used to him being around. Now, five years later, Toby is happy and healthy, and has grown to 45 pounds, eating anything and everything (including cat food). In fact, he needs to go on a diet!

Toby's story is just one of many heartbreaking stories from Hurricane Katrina. Sadly, dogs such as Toby are found in every city, even those that haven't experienced such dire circumstances.

- Susan and Scott Glassman

Wallace

Wallace is an unusual mix. We're guessing he is a mix of pit bull, Labrador retriever, and greyhound. Whatever he is, he's a great dog! I adopted Wallace when he was two years old from Palmetto Animal League in Okatie, SC. I already had Bailey, who was then three years old, and was adopted from where I attended technical school.

Wallace was meant to be my dog. I am a veterinary technician and was working at a veterinary hospital when Wallace (then called Oscar) was brought in for treatment. He had been placed in a foster home through Palmetto Animal League and had run away, too scared for anyone to catch him. Several of his rescuers spent many days and nights trying to catch him, and even brought in a trainer. Apparently he was stealing lawn ornaments and shoes from the neighbors' porches and the community's security had threatened to shoot him. The community's security team called in animal control, which over-tranquilized Wallace to catch him, and it took days for him to regain consciousness. While taking care of him, I became very attached and we decided to adopt him. The adoption experience was a good one. We love Wallace, and everyone who had met him was very happy to see him finally find his forever home.

Everybody at the veterinary hospital felt horrible about his situation. On his third day of hospitalization with us we had to bathe him. He was conscious, but could not stand up or walk on his own. I held his head up while we washed him and I knew then, looking into his sad eyes, I was going to take him home.

I was told that he was found as a feral dog. He is still nervous and unsure about many things. It took us months after we adopted him just to get him to walk down the hallway and go into the bedrooms. He has come a long way. He still does not wag his tail; only on rare occasions when he is playing in the yard with his sister. He has very thoughtful eyes. He is quiet and always looks concerned about something or deep in thought. He is a very unique dog.

Our family continues to grow, as we recently adopted another dog from Palmetto Animal League. Ellie is a 10-month-old pit bull. It's so tempting to adopt these wonderful dogs since I now work for Palmetto Animal League as a veterinary technician and operations manager.

- Lori Mihalcik

Webster

We adopted Webster, a bassett hound/Labrador retriever mix, when he was just a 10-week-old puppy. We didn't have any other dogs at that time and it was our first experience adopting a dog. It was quite simple, really. We wanted a dog and went to the Frederick County Animal Control in Frederick, MD, and there he was.

Actually he wasn't what we were looking for. I went to the shelter to look at dogs, not puppies. I was not sure I was ready for this experience, as I had lost a dog just eight months prior to visiting the shelter. My heart was still aching for her. Then my friend had me look at the puppies, and there was Webster, such a funny looking little dude. I was allowed to hold him and he smothered me with kisses, making funny little noises. No need to look further. I was hooked.

The adoption experience was good in every way. We will most likely adopt a dog the next time we bring in a new family member.

Webster has been a very loving and outgoing dog from the beginning, with many funny quirks. He loves "bobos," which is our word for stuffed toys. He parades them all over the house, licks them, plays fetch with them, and pulls the stuffing and squeakers out of them. When he's not playing, he is busy being a loving lap dog. He bonded immediately with my husband's aunt, who lived with us for two years. After she went into a nursing home, we had to take him to see her or he would pace and whine. When she died, we took him to see her. He got up on her bed and laid his head on her hand. After that, he never whined to see her again. Dogs are so smart and know so much more than we give them credit for. We're so glad to have Webster in our lives to entertain, comfort and love us!

- Brenda Cook

Titan and his Cousins

Titan

Maggie

Motley

Sasha